Practical Buddhism for Modern Life

Key Buddhist Teachings to Help Women Get Through Their Days

Priya Roshan

© **Copyright 2023 - All rights reserved.**

The content contained within this book may not be reproduced, duplicated or transmitted without direct written permission from the author or the publisher.

Under no circumstances will any blame or legal responsibility be held against the publisher, or author, for any damages, reparation, or monetary loss due to the information contained within this book, either directly or indirectly.

Legal Notice:

This book is copyright protected. It is only for personal use. You cannot amend, distribute, sell, use, quote or paraphrase any part, or the content within this book, without the consent of the author or publisher.

Disclaimer Notice:

Please note the information contained within this document is for educational and entertainment purposes only. All effort has been executed to present accurate, up to date, reliable, complete information. No warranties of any kind are declared or implied. Readers acknowledge that the author is not engaged in the rendering of legal, financial, medical or professional advice. The content within this book has been derived from various sources. Please consult a licensed professional before attempting any techniques outlined in this book.

By reading this document, the reader agrees that under no circumstances is the author responsible for any losses, direct or indirect, that are incurred as a result of the use of the information contained within this document, including, but not limited to, errors, omissions, or inaccuracies.

Author's Disclaimer:

The information and practices included in this book exist solely in relation to modern Buddhism. Any actions or opinions expressed outside of this work, by those who are referenced, are separate from the author's intentions.

Table of Contents

TABLE OF CONTENTS 5

INTRODUCTION 1

CHAPTER 1: AN INTRODUCTION TO BUDDHISM 7
- BUDDHA 8
- BUDDHIST PHILOSOPHY 10
    - *The Four Noble Truths* *11*
    - *Life, Death, and Rebirth* *13*
- MEDITATION AND MINDFULNESS 15
- WOMEN AND BUDDHISM 18
- INCORPORATING BUDDHISM INTO YOUR EVERYDAY LIFE 21

CHAPTER 2: FINDING HAPPINESS 23
- THE BUDDHIST VIEW OF HAPPINESS 25
    - *Happiness and Joy* *25*
    - *Attachment Inhibits Joy* *26*
    - *Can Anyone Be Happy?* *28*
    - *The Importance of Community* *34*
- EXERCISES FOR JOYFULNESS 36
    - *Mindfulness Practices* *36*
    - *Belly Breathing* *39*
    - *Tsoknyi Rinpoche's "Dropping" Technique* *40*
    - *Setting Intentions* *42*

CHAPTER 3: LIVING FREELY 45
- THE NOTION OF FREE WILL 45
- MENTAL FREEDOM 48
    - *The Wisdom of Thich Nhat Hanh* *49*
- EXERCISES FOR FREEDOM 50
    - *Practice Authenticity* *50*
    - *Think Before Speaking and Acting* *52*
    - *Freedom In Every Smile* *54*

CHAPTER 4: ACTING WITH COMPASSION 57
- THE COMPONENTS OF COMPASSION 58

    Solidarity 59
    Forgiveness 61
    Gratitude 62
    Self-Compassion 63
  Exercises for Compassion 64
    Gratitude Practice 64
    Forgiveness Practice 65
    Karuna Meditation 67
    Mani Mantra 69

CHAPTER 5: WELCOMING DIFFICULT EMOTIONS 71
  Difficult Emotions Serve a Purpose 72
  Suffering Stems From Reactivity 73
  Exercises for Diffusing Negativity 74
    Breathing Exercises for Anxiety and Stress 74
    Atlas of Emotions 76
    Grief Meditation 77
    Shake Hands With Your Beautiful Monsters 78

CHAPTER 6: CHOOSING TO REST 83
  Give Yourself a Break 83
  Procrastination and Distraction 85
  Exercises for Rest 90
    Yoga Nidra 90
    Methods for Better Sleep 93
    Stepping Away From Your Devices 96

CONCLUSION 99

GLOSSARY 103

THANK YOU 107

ABOUT THE AUTHOR 107

REFERENCES 109

Introduction

If there is one undeniable, universal truth for humanity, it is that life is challenging. It does not matter who you are, where you live, or how much money you have in your bank account. Everyone will experience difficult moments during their time on Earth. This may be a disappointing, or even painful, idea to accept, but there is an upside. With every challenge that life throws your way, there is beauty. Time and again, people have shown resilience and optimism in the face of suffering. Humans have the unique ability to learn from their hardships, accept their circumstances, and move forward, finding peace in the madness. To live in peace is to accept that challenges are inevitable.

Think back on the last few years leading up to this moment. Unless you live in a fantasy world where everything is rainbows and butterflies, you have probably experienced some of the hardest moments of your life. You may have learned what it means to be pushed to your breaking point. You may have felt lost, misunderstood, or utterly detached from your purpose. More than likely, you have felt the inexplicable confusion and fear of living through difficult world events. Your life has undoubtedly been touched by loss and grief in a variety of ways.

Yet, here you are. Despite the suffering you have endured, recently or in the distant past, you survived. Now, you can take the necessary steps to move forward and be truly happy. You may be thinking: *How am I supposed to do that when I'm so busy with everything else in my life?* Whether you work a demanding job, take care of a hectic family, study endlessly for your dream degree or certification—or a combination of all three—know that you can live a life that feels peaceful, productive, and purposeful.

This is where Buddhism comes in. If you are unfamiliar with the term, Buddhism is a philosophy centered around the understanding and acceptance of suffering to achieve enlightenment and happiness. For millennia, people all over the world have practiced the teachings of the Buddha, balancing their challenges and happiness. The beliefs and lessons that stem from Buddhism may be considered ancient, but they are just as beneficial today as they were centuries ago, maybe even more so. With all of the stressors that exist for modern women—like parenting, juggling a career and family, patriarchal societies, and gender discrimination—practicing Buddhism can be life-changing.

Practical Buddhism for Modern Life is an insightful guide to the Buddha's lessons, filled with realistic exercises you can use every day. Using clear and straightforward language, this book offers women the tools they need to live a more mindful and fulfilling life. Bringing Buddhist practices into your life does not have to mean completely overthrowing your current religious or spiritual beliefs either. Applying even the easiest or least time-consuming exercises to your daily routine can improve your well-being.

In the following chapters, you will be given an in-depth look at what it means to be a student of the Buddha. From learning the Buddhist perspective of happiness and joy to understanding how to befriend your more difficult thoughts and emotions, this book will guide you through the core teachings of the ancient philosophy. Every chapter will provide you with various practices to implement in your everyday life, including meditations, affirmations, breathing exercises, and more. Drawing insight from the author's own research and life experiences, as well as countless lessons from acclaimed Buddhist teachers, *Practical Buddhism for Modern Life* is bursting with invaluable wisdom.

However, before you can dive into the knowledge held within these pages, you must first understand how Buddhism came to be. As with most important lessons, a sturdy foundation must be established before any enlightenment can be achieved. That is why the first chapter of this book is dedicated to the history of Buddhism and the life of its founder, Siddhartha Gautama. Famously known as "the Buddha," Siddhartha Gautama spent his life discovering the true meaning of enlightenment. His origins are as important to understanding Buddhist teachings as the lessons themselves. Once you have a solid grasp of the early history of Buddhism, you will be ready to accept the wisdom of this book.

In the second chapter, you will learn what it means to be happy from a Buddhist perspective. The Buddha's outlook on happiness may look very different from what you have sought throughout your life. According to the Buddha, true joy does not come from a successful career, the building of a family, or a bank account filled with more money than you can spend. While these things may bring moments of excitement and warmth to your life, true joy comes from within. Chapter 2 will teach you how to cultivate genuine happiness in your life without encouraging you to seek a lifestyle you do not currently have. You will learn that you already have every tool you need to live a life that brings you joy.

Chapter 3 introduces the ideas of free will and mental freedom, two notions that are deeply intertwined in Buddhism. In this chapter, you will learn the difference between free will and determinism, as well as the middle-ground concept that many Buddhist practitioners abide by. The phenomenon of Karma will be discussed concerning one's free will and ability to design their life path, and you will identify the power that arises when you free yourself from emotional restrictions.

Once you learn about true mental freedom, you will be introduced to the root of Buddhism: compassion. Compassionate action, which is discussed at length in Chapter 4, is the antidote to discontentment that you have been searching for. By learning about and practicing compassion toward yourself and others, you will rid your mind of the negativity that plagues it. This chapter will teach you all about the components of compassion and provide you with realistic, transformative practices that will help you cultivate compassion in your daily life.

In Chapter 5, you will learn the truth about the negative things you feel every day. You may be so overwhelmed by anger, frustration, sadness, or exhaustion to the point where you feel that nothing can be done to alleviate the emotional burden. When you feel this way, it can seem as though your only choice is to live in a bubble of negativity. Chapter 5 is here to show you that this is not your destiny. You are made for so much love and happiness; you simply have not yet been taught how to develop those feelings amid such pain. Though Buddhism is not a cure for mental illness, its teachings can help you develop a better mindset as you navigate the world of emotional healing.

Finally, after learning the ins and outs of emotional well-being and spiritual healing, you will arrive at Chapter 6. Here you will be encouraged to rest your mind, body, and spirit so that you can regain your energy and experience everything life has to offer. This chapter will teach you about the importance of giving yourself a break and provide you with several methods to do so. Whether you are a sleep-deprived mom, an insomniac with too many worries, or just a woman who has trouble stepping away from her cell phone, Chapter 6 will help you rest.

Overall, the goal of this book is to let you know that your busy life and overwhelming emotions do not have to bring you suffering. With the help of Buddhist wisdom and practices, you can overcome the challenges in your everyday life and come out to the other side feeling joyful and inspired.

Chapter 1:

An Introduction to Buddhism

Buddhism is considered many things: faith, philosophy, religion, and even a state of mind. Regardless of what it's called, it is a belief system that has changed the lives of billions of people since its inception. Buddhism has existed for over 2,000 years, making it one of the oldest religions to still be practiced in the 21st century (Jank, 2022). Somewhere between the sixth and fourth centuries BCE, the teachings of the Buddha were developed and spread throughout Asia before they reached the Western society.

Today, it is believed that there are over 470 million followers of Buddhism. This is an incredible amount of people, all dedicated to learning from the teachings of the Buddha. Moreover, this number only includes those who actively practice the religion and claim to be Buddhist. It does not take into account the innumerable amount of people that partake in Buddhist practices every day without even knowing it. Anyone who meditates, practices mindfulness, or simply uses the term *zen* is dabbling in Buddhism. But how did this widespread, centuries-long philosophy come to be? Well, it all started with a man named Siddhartha Gautama.

Buddha

Siddhartha Gautama was born a prince in the Sakya Kingdom, a territory that was located in what we now know as Nepal.

Prince Siddhartha, as he was known in his younger years, was heavily sheltered and protected by his royal parents. According to scholars, a prediction was made during Siddhartha's birth, stating he would ultimately fulfill one of two fates. The young prince would either become a king, like his father, or a Buddha. That is, Siddhartha would follow a path of spiritual enlightenment while teaching others how to do the same. The prediction declared that the only way the prince would become a ruler was if he was protected from pain and suffering. Wanting his son to become a great ruler, the king kept Siddhartha away from the outside world.

For more than two decades, the king's efforts to shelter the prince were successful. Siddhartha was only exposed to life's greatest luxuries and experiences. He never witnessed or experienced significant suffering, and he had infinite access to material treasures. Once he came of age, the prince got married and had a son of his own. Siddhartha's fate seemed obvious to the king.

However, when he was 29 years old, Prince Siddhartha began exploring the land outside the safety of his royal home. He had a chariot take him around the kingdom to observe what life was like for the common people. Throughout his various trips away from his palace, Siddhartha saw how people were suffering. He saw the sick, the poor, the dead, and the dying. Having been sheltered from these misfortunes for so long, Siddhartha's chariot driver had to explain to him what was happening. The prince learned that pain and suffering were common aspects of everyday life, and he had simply been hidden from them.

Siddhartha eventually met a monk while exploring the outside world and was surprised by the man's serene outlook on life. Siddhartha could not understand how the monk could have such inner peace among so much distress and agony. This idea inspired the prince to continue his adventures away from his palace, hoping to reach the same level of peace as the monk.

After renouncing his royal lifestyle and the riches it guaranteed, Siddhartha Gautama spent his time as an ascetic. This meant that he would completely separate himself from the extravagances of society, like ornate materials and pleasurable activities, to focus on his spirituality. He learned the wisdom of two teachers in South Asia, Alara Kalama and Udraka Ramaputra, who helped him reach "high states of mystical realization" (History.com Editors, 2020b). Though he mastered the teachings and learned to meditate successfully, Siddhartha was left wanting more from his spiritual endeavors. He felt he had not yet reached true enlightenment, a state of mind known as *nirvana*. Because of this dissatisfaction, the prince-turned-monk sought an even stricter, more ascetic lifestyle. Siddhartha fasted, practiced lengthy meditations, and lived in extreme poverty for years.

Once again, Siddhartha was unsatisfied with his life of self-discipline, feeling that it was not an effective method for achieving nirvana. At this point in his journey, he had experienced both being a wealthy prince and a devoted monk living without material possessions. Neither existence had given him the inner clarity he was after. Thus, Siddhartha decided on the Middle Way, a philosophy that endorses an avoidance of the two extremes. Instead of subjecting oneself to severe restriction and poverty nor becoming dependent on life's indulgences, the Middle Way lights a path in between.

Under a tree in India, meditating on his newfound wisdom, Siddhartha reached nirvana. He was officially a Buddha.

Buddhist Philosophy

The Gautama Buddha, to which he is often referred, began teaching others about his way of life. He encouraged them to seek enlightenment for themselves through the core methods of the Middle Way. As scholars of Buddhism have reported, the Buddha gave his first sermon at a deer park in India (The Pluralism Project, 2023). He taught his listeners the meaning of his philosophy, including the Four Noble Truths; the Noble Eightfold Path; what it means to live, die, and be reborn; the existence of karma; and the importance of meditation.

In its simplest form, the Buddha's philosophy is a series of steps one must take to achieve total enlightenment. Buddhism acknowledges the necessity and inevitability of suffering in life and provides a trusted way to end such suffering. To the followers of Buddhism, these truths are known as *Dharma*.

To practice Buddhism, one must participate in three types of training. Firstly, a true Buddhist will practice *sila*. This means they will have good morals and treat others as their equals, giving when they can and having compassion. Secondly, the Buddha's followers will train in *samadhi*, the act of developing one's mindset through deep concentration and meditation. Finally, Buddhists will develop *prajna*, the wisdom and enlightened awareness of the Buddha.

As practitioners of Buddhist philosophy train in these three ideals, they will trust in the Four Noble Truths.

The Four Noble Truths

The Four Noble Truths of Buddhism reveal the truth and purpose of human suffering. The first Noble Truth is straightforward: suffering is, and always will, exist in the world. In Sanskrit, the word *duhkha* is used to represent suffering and unhappiness. To the Buddha, there is no human existence without pain and suffering.

The second Noble Truth is that all suffering has a cause; it is not meaningless or uncontrollable. This concept is represented by the Sanskrit word *samudaya*. For Buddhists, the cause of suffering is one's "desire to have or control things" (UNHCR, 2012). Samudaya can stem from the avoidance of painful emotions or experiences, one's attachment to luxuries, or even one's hope that suffering may never occur.

The third Noble Truth explains that, although suffering will always exist, it can be overcome. This Noble Truth describes the goal of reaching nirvana, through which one can free themselves from suffering and attachment. The word *nirodha*, in Sanskrit, represents this truth.

The fourth Noble Truth, represented by the word *magga*, is that a certain path must be followed to overcome suffering and become enlightened. This path is considered the Eightfold Path.

The Eightfold Path

The path discussed in the fourth Noble Truth serves as a set of achievable steps for Buddhist practitioners to follow. The Eightfold Path describes actions one can take within each of the three types of Buddhist training (UNHCR, 2012). The Eightfold Path consists of the following ideals:

- Right Understanding: To accept the Four Noble Truths.

- Right Intention (sometimes referred to as Right Aspiration): To follow a life path that is free from desire, self-indulgence, and ignorance.

- Right Speech: To avoid speaking with hatred, lies, criticism, and harsh language.

- Right Action (sometimes referred to as Right Conduct): To live without exhibiting harmful or hurtful behaviors, such as violence, careless physical relations, and theft.

- Right Livelihood: To make a living for and support oneself without harming others, including animals.

- Right Effort: To think according to the right values by overcoming bad thoughts and sustaining good thoughts.

- Right Mindfulness: To remain in tune with your mind, body, and spirit to overcome negativity.

- Right Concentration: To practice meditation and make progress toward enlightenment.

Because Buddhism is practiced all over the world, there are various interpretations of the Eightfold Path. Different cultures in different areas practice Buddhism in their own unique ways. That being said, most interpretations come from the same basic understanding that a person must have good morals, good intentions, and good practices to reach nirvana.

The Four Noble Truths and Eightfold Path provide Buddhists with a clear guide to living a fulfilling life. By following the Buddha's teachings, one can grow their consciousness to the highest level. This evolved mindset not only allows one to accept that being alive means experiencing painful situations but also to find peace in the present moment. In a world full of suffering, it is instinctual to fear and mourn our losses. The core philosophy of Buddhism emphasizes the importance of releasing these difficult emotions and embracing life's inevitability. The only aspect of life that can be controlled is how one responds to moments of suffering.

Life, Death, and Rebirth

Those who practice the teachings of the Buddha also believe in a specific cycle of human life. Buddhists acknowledge a continuous cycle that can only end when a person has achieved total enlightenment. Before that happens, *if* it happens, a person will endure several lives and several deaths. After each lifetime, they will die and be reborn into a new life, beginning the cycle over again.

With each life a person lives, they will have the chance to accept the Four Noble Truths and work toward their own enlightenment. Pain and suffering will be endured, as they are inevitable aspects of the human condition, but there may also be moments of happiness and satisfaction. The cycle of life, death, and rebirth—known to Buddhists as *samsara*—will continue forever until one has dedicated their existence to enlightening their mindset. As soon as they can accept the role of suffering and follow the Buddhist philosophy successfully, they will achieve the purest form of joy and satisfaction, thus ending their cycle and bringing them to nirvana.

Karma

This life cycle does, however, come with a condition called *karma*. Though it is a common word in modern Western society, many people are unaware of the true meaning of karma. Through his spiritual endeavors, the Buddha discovered that a person's behaviors and intentions during one lifetime will dictate their experience in future lifetimes. For example, if a person acts out of hatred and violence throughout their life, they will endure more suffering in their next life as a consequence.

On the other end of the spectrum, if a person acts mercifully and with good intentions, they will be rewarded with more moments of joy, rather than pain, in their next life. Naturally, this concept encourages believers to behave according to the Buddha's teachings so that they may experience the positive side of karma in the future.

Meditation and Mindfulness

The teachings of Buddhism are best understood through intense contemplation. In other words, the ancient philosophy is rooted in meditation. The practice of meditation is certainly not unheard of in modern Western societies, even in those that do not abide by Buddhist values. You may read the word *meditation* and immediately imagine a person sitting cross-legged with their palms on their knees, eyes closed peacefully. You may have even practiced meditation yourself, as part of a class, or on your own. Meditation has become an increasingly common practice, particularly among those who are passionate about spiritualism and self-healing.

Similar to the concept of karma, however, meditation holds profound significance in Buddhist training, a fact that is often overlooked. In addition to its calming benefits, meditation has been used for thousands of years to evoke self-awareness and a spiritual connection to the universe. Meditating allows a person to become more mindful of their physical and emotional experience, as well as their environment. By practicing mindfulness through meditation, one can focus on the truths that lie beyond human existence. The Buddha underwent countless hours of meditation to achieve his enlightenment and taught others to do the same. The act of sitting in a meditative state is often referred to as *shamatha*, a Sanskrit word meaning tranquility and peaceful abiding.

The idea that one can practice spirituality and connectedness simply by sitting quietly may seem far-fetched, but it is truly a transformative activity. Of course, a meditative practice every few weeks may not result in Buddha-level enlightenment. It takes immense dedication to Buddhist philosophy to achieve such nirvana. However, it is possible to reap the many benefits of meditation after just a handful of attempts.

Though the physical act is not very complex, the mental endeavor can be challenging. The human brain is wired to produce rapid, conflicting thoughts. Because of this, getting those thoughts to settle down for one minute, let alone one hour, can feel like an impossible task. Thus, it is crucial to concentrate on breathing, especially for beginners. By focusing on the ebb and flow of your breath, your mind will naturally put your thoughts and concerns to rest, at least for a moment. The more this concentration is practiced, the easier it will become to turn your focus to your breathing rather than your preoccupations. When you do this, you give yourself room to harness your inner peace.

World-renowned Buddhist monk, Thich Nhat Hanh, has provided the world with incredible insight into meditation and mindfulness practices. Before his passing in early 2022, Thich Nhat Hanh wrote about what it means to be mindful through meditation: "The object of your mindfulness is your breath, and you just focus your attention on it...You don't think of the past anymore. You don't think of the future" (Thich, 2023b). Giving yourself permission to exist only in the present moment will help you release any fears, worries, or regrets you may have. Even if your meditation practice only lasts for a few minutes, you will feel the weight of your thoughts being lifted from your shoulders.

The act of meditating does not require much. Some people choose to use specific pieces of furniture for sitting on, such as a meditation stool, but it is not imperative to the practice. What is most important is that you meditate in a safe, serene place, one that you feel comfortable in. This can be a calming room in your home, a quiet location in nature, or anywhere else. Susan Piver, a published author and meditation instructor, teaches that meditating at the same time each day can also benefit one's practice (Piver, 2008).

Wherever and whenever you meditate, make sure your mind and body are at ease. It is recommended by many Buddhist teachers to sit with your legs loosely crossed, especially if you are sitting on a cushion or directly on the floor. If you are in a chair or on a couch, sit with your feet flat on the floor or ground beneath you. In both positions, you should maintain your posture by keeping your spine as straight as you comfortably can. Slouching or hunching your shoulders forward can impair your breathing, which can disrupt your entire practice. The breath is the focus of the mind during meditation, so it is important to allow your breathing to be as free and uninhibited as possible.

While you breathe, be sure to focus for the entire length of your breaths, however long they may be. Thich Nhat Hanh wrote that while your breaths can be short or long, you must follow them from beginning to end. During meditation, your mindfulness lasts the duration of each breath, both inward and outward. "From the beginning of my out-breath to the end of my out-breath," Thich Nhat Hanh wrote, "my mind is always with it" (Thich, 2023b). By following each breath as it enters and exits your body, you limit the opportunities for your mind to interrupt with distracting thoughts.

You may struggle with your concentration during your first attempts at meditating. For many people, focusing on breathing for an extended period of time is a difficult skill to master, so don't be too hard on yourself if you become distracted or get interrupted. Consistent practice will help, and it may come with a feeling of great accomplishment. If you are meditating for the first time or have not practiced for a while, begin with short meditations. As little as two to five minutes of meditation and mindfulness is enough to start your journey. Over time, you can lengthen your practices as much as you'd like. On that same note, the breaths you take during your meditations do not need to last a certain amount of time if that is difficult for you. Do what feels natural and comfortable in the moment—think of that as a mindfulness practice of its own.

In the following chapters, you will be given various opportunities to practice what you have now learned about meditation and mindfulness. With each practice, remember the core concepts of shamatha: find a safe, comfortable place to sit; try to meditate at the same time each day; focus on each breath; and concentrate on the present moment.

Women and Buddhism

Around 2,500 years ago, when the Buddha began his spiritual journey, much of the world discriminated against women. Various religions at the time prioritized the male perspective on spirituality, while women were often overlooked. Outside of religion, women were frequently encouraged to obey their fathers and husbands, making men the dominant gender. Granted, women were appreciated for their form and femininity, and ancient religions like Hinduism and Judaism discuss the existence of female goddesses, so women were not completely ignored at the time. However, it was rare for ordinary, human women to be viewed as individuals, independent from the men in their lives. That is until the Buddha sparked controversy with his beliefs.

Researchers have long debated the role of feminism in relation to Buddhist philosophy—some say that the introduction of Buddhism was revolutionary for female empowerment, while others believe the Buddha maintained a preference for men over women (Sirimanne, 2016). Nonetheless, there is no disagreement that Buddhism was one of the first recognized religions to emphasize the importance of women in societal, familial, and spiritual roles.

Because the Buddha believed in treating all people as equals, it makes sense that this would include women. He encouraged his followers, regardless of their gender, to respect each other as they themselves would want to be respected. Though the Buddha was a man, he did not believe himself to be better than anyone, in any regard, especially in gender. Ancient Buddhist texts reveal that the Buddha called for equal rights between men and women, a unique facet of his philosophy. This equality extended into the spiritual realm, as the Buddha strongly believed that women should follow a religious path in the same way as men. The women who chose this path and dedicated their entire lives to it, like monks, were called *bhikkhunis*, or *nuns*.

One article featured on the website Feminism in India reports that the Buddha's achievement of nirvana relied on the inclusion of women. The article quotes the Buddha, stating: "I will not take final Nirvana until I have nuns and female disciples who are accomplished" (Bhattacharya, 2017). By saying this, the Buddha revealed to the world that his life goal, his entire purpose, depended on the inclusion of women in his teachings. His desire to help others reach enlightenment was not hindered by gender disparities or socio-economic beliefs; enlightenment is for everyone to work toward.

Dhammananda Bhikkhuni, a renowned Buddhist nun from Thailand, has spoken at length about what it means to be a woman who practices Buddhism. In an interview from 2021, Dhammananda Bhikkhuni emphasized the importance of having female monks with active roles in Buddhist practices. She discussed her choice to divorce her husband and pursue a life of celibacy and religion, as well as her perspective on putting her children first before committing to a new life path. Once her children had grown into adults, she felt that her time had come to enter a more spiritual chapter in her life.

When asked for her opinion on feminism and equality, Dhamananda Bhikkhuni described the Buddha as the first feminist due to his adamant inclusion and protection of his female students. She explained that, from her perspective, feminism "means a woman can do whatever she has the potential to do" (Rasicot, 2021). Feminism in Buddhist practices, in particular, means fighting for the right of women to become masters of the Buddha's teachings in the same way that men are encouraged to do so.

Incorporating Buddhism Into Your Everyday Life

The purpose of this book is to provide you with practical, achievable methods through which you can benefit from Buddhist philosophy every day. Though the foundation of Buddhism is based on intense commitment and dedication to the teachings, you are encouraged to implement the teachings of this book however you please. There is no need to pressure yourself into upheaving the entire structure of your life to abide by Buddhist values. Rather, allow the teachings in this book to guide you through your days in moments when you need encouragement. You certainly do not have to aspire to become a Buddhist teacher or nun to benefit from the following lessons.

If you are a busy mother, you may choose to apply the Buddhist philosophy to your parenting style or in moments when you are utterly overwhelmed with familial responsibilities. If you are stretched thin at your job, you may use Buddhist techniques to recenter yourself and find a sense of peace among the stress. If you are a student working tirelessly toward higher education, the lessons in this book may encourage a balanced mindset and a sense of purpose. For some, Buddhism may lend a helping hand in all of these aspects of life in different ways.

Every woman has experienced life's challenges. To be female in this world is to look hardship in the eye and fight for a life you love. Despite being criticized, patronized, and underestimated, women can and do have the power to find happiness, and this book is here to help you do just that.

Chapter 2:

Finding Happiness

There have, undoubtedly, been times in your life when you have questioned your own happiness. It may have been in a small way, such as choosing one event over another. You may have thought, *would I have been happier doing something else?* It may have been in a bigger way—perhaps you were unsure of the career path you chose or the relationship you were in. Questioning whether or not your current situation is making you happiest is completely normal; however, your doubts should not bring you stress or pain.

Being happy is both simple and complex. On the one hand, you can find happiness by following your heart and making decisions that feel authentic to you. On the other hand, staying true to yourself for the sake of happiness can come at a cost. The decisions you make in the pursuit of your own fulfillment may lead you to make major life changes, ones that can be challenging and distressing to make. That is one of the reasons why so many people settle for lifestyles that do not truly make them happy. They may be satisfied with their choices, sometimes even pleased by them. But deep down, they know they are not as happy as they could be because they are afraid to make difficult choices.

So, what happens then? Do these almost-happy people live the rest of their lives doubting their emotional state? For some, this may be the case. Living with such doubt can be overwhelming. When happiness feels like a distant goal rather than a nearby possibility, you begin to grasp at straws to satisfy yourself.

How many times have you purchased, planned, or done something in the hope that it will make you happier? It isn't anything to be ashamed of; we've all done it. The instant gratification that comes with a new material item or experience gives our brains an emotional boost, making us feel happy. Instant gratification, though, only lasts for a few moments. Science has proven that our brain has two conflicting parts: one logical and one emotional (Chu, 2017). Our emotional brain is what acts on impulse, especially when positive rewards are involved.

Imagine there is a table in front of you, and on that table are two plates of food. The plate on the left is piled high with raw vegetables, and the plate on the right is full of your absolute favorite desserts. For most people—that is, those who would prefer their favorite dessert over vegetables—the emotional side of their brain will tell them to grab the plate of sweet treats. This emotional, impulsive side of the brain wants the instant gratification of having its preferred snack, knowing it will feel pleasure. The logical side, however, will probably try to rationalize grabbing the plate of healthy vegetables because of their nutritional value.

Though this is a low-stakes example, its meaning applies to much more significant circumstances. The emotional and logical sides of the human brain fight each other over most decisions. When someone is desperate to feel happy, even if only for a moment, the emotional side of their brain will be more attracted to the choice that gives them instant gratification. While this can feel good, it is not the most sustainable method for achieving true happiness.

The Buddhist View of Happiness

Happiness and Joy

The first thing you must understand about the Buddhist view of happiness is that the terms *happiness* and *joy* are not interchangeable. They may seem like two words with the same meaning, but they are not. The Dalai Lama, the foremost spiritual leader of Tibetan Buddhism, connects the word *happiness* with an impermanent feeling of sensory satisfaction, as explained in *The Book of Joy* (Lama et al., 2016). Feelings of happiness tend to come from external pleasures, like food, music, or physical experiences. These things can make someone feel happy in the moment, which is not a bad thing, but they do not last as long as true joyfulness.

Joy is an all-encompassing feeling, more of a state of mind than a singular emotion. Within joy, there is happiness, compassion, gratitude, and satisfaction all at once. Feeling joyful comes from the inside, not from external measures. It consists of a deep feeling of inner peace and fulfillment, making it last much longer than a fleeting sense of happiness. By reaching nirvana, the Buddha was able to experience the truest form of joy.

It could be argued that, by filling one's life with enough happiness, one could experience joy. This may be possible to some extent, but it depends on the person's inner state. Even with all of the material or sensory pleasures in the world, building up thousands of moments of brief happiness, joy will not be found until the mental state is completely fulfilled. The Dalai Lama says that no amount of "physical comforts or pleasure" will create true joy if a person's mind is still preoccupied with fears and worries.

Attachment Inhibits Joy

From a Buddhist perspective, joy comes from one's lack of attachment. This word, *attachment,* is referenced frequently in different Buddhist teachings and scriptures. To be attached means you are clinging to one specific idea, emotion, material item, or lifestyle. This does not mean you are physically connected, but rather that you are desperate for the idea, emotion, material item, or lifestyle to remain constant. You want to have control over what stays in or out of your life. When you then realize you do not have control—that realization is inevitable—you experience pain, grief, and suffering.

Take the concept of love, for example. A loving relationship can bring out one's most positive emotions. Being in love makes you feel satisfied and cared for. With those positive emotions, though, comes the fear of losing them. One becomes so attached to the idea of being in love and so distraught at the idea of losing that love, that one is unable to feel truly happy. There is always that small worry in the back of their mind that something will ruin the positive experience they have built.

Thus, one tries to control as much as one possibly can. They may work tirelessly to control your emotional state by pushing away the negative thoughts; they may try to control their partner's safety by never letting them out of sight; or maybe they try to prevent themselves from getting hurt by self-sabotaging, ultimately hurting everyone involved. They are so attached to the idea of remaining in love or remaining unhurt that they cannot experience true happiness in their relationship.

The antidote to attachment is acceptance. When you can accept that suffering is inevitable, as Buddhism teaches, you will learn to appreciate what you have when you have it. You will begin to see that being so attached and desperate for control will get you nowhere since life is uncontrollable. It can be an incredibly difficult idea to accept. Most people do not want to imagine that they will suffer or that they will witness the suffering of their loved ones. It's much easier to hope that suffering is avoidable if you do certain things or live a certain way. Yet, easier does not always mean better. As long as you have the desire to control the uncontrollable, including your own emotions, you will never truly be happy.

The Dalai Lama teaches that "once there is attachment, there is also the potential for anger and hatred to arise" (The 14th Dalai Lama, 2022). By saying this, the Dalai Lama implies that being attached to a certain outcome or feeling leaves a greater opportunity for disappointment and, thus, negativity. If you are expecting to feel one way as a result of your attachment and that expectation is not met, you may feel even worse than if you had simply accepted that whatever happens, happens.

Herein lies the first step to finding joy, according to the Buddha. You must not seek only the best feelings, like satisfaction or pleasure. In fact, you must try not to seek anything. In the same way that whatever happens in life will happen regardless of your attempt to control it, whatever emotions arise in you will arise. By purposely seeking out good feelings, you will only end up experiencing the bad feelings more intensely. All you need to do is accept that everything that happens to and within you will happen no matter what. Accept all of your feelings as they arise.

If your negative emotions are of major concern to you, don't worry. The fifth chapter of this book will go into more detail on how these feelings can benefit us and contribute to our joy.

Can Anyone Be Happy?

At this point, you may be wondering how the process of cultivating joy can sound so simple yet be so complex. It is certainly not as easy as saying, "I now accept everything as it is and I will be joyful." Finding joy is a skill that requires patience and practice. First, you must take the time to process the meaning of being joyful. You must truly understand the difference between impermanent happiness and inner peace. Allow yourself time to consider what you have read and let it sink in. You do not need to rush yourself into finding your joy.

Remember, the Buddha spent nearly three decades in blissful ignorance as a prince. He was not born enlightened, nor did he develop his own beliefs the moment he witnessed suffering for the first time. The Buddha took his time cultivating his joy. He put in hours of spiritual and mental work in order to reach nirvana. And that was before social media, nine-to-five jobs, and all of the other new-age developments of the 21st century. Every day you are bombarded with new information to process and new responsibilities to manage. Simply put, your life is most likely overwhelming enough as it is. There is no need for you to attach yourself to the idea that you must develop inner peace at this very second. It will take time.

Once you have given yourself time to understand the importance of freeing yourself from attachment, you can delve deeper into the components of inner peace. Buddhists believe that the joy that comes from inner peace consists of a handful of emotional skills: generosity, kindness, altruism, empathy, and compassion. By living with these skills as your core values, you purify your mind of self-involvement and attachment.

Generosity

Generosity is the practice of giving to others, typically without expecting anything in return. This does not just mean giving material items, such as gifts or money. While doing so can be a generous act, you can express your generosity in many more ways. Teaching, supporting, and lending a helping hand to others are all intangible ways of being generous. Donating your time and wholehearted attention is just as valuable as giving them a physical donation.

To be generous, you must free yourself from feelings of greed and reciprocity. Buddhist philosophy emphasizes the significance of giving without expectation or attachment to a reward. For example, while donating your time to volunteer at a charity would be considered generous, it would be less generous if you were volunteering only to receive something beneficial in return. True generosity comes from your willingness to contribute to someone else's well-being purely because you want them to be well. The more you practice true generosity, the more it purifies your mind and creates an overall generous spirit within you.

The Buddha practiced generosity throughout his spiritual journey in many ways, though most significantly by imparting his wisdom to others and encouraging their own enlightenment. He did not withhold his teachings in order to keep them for himself. He gave others his time and attention to cultivate his generous spirit. By doing so, he purified his mind and got closer to reaching nirvana.

Kindness

You may be well acquainted with kindness already. It is a concept that is instilled in many people from a young age. For Buddhists, it is a critical part of becoming enlightened. Practicing kindness means you do not act from a place of hatred, discrimination, or anger. To be kind, you must relinquish your attachment to those negative feelings and act with good intentions. It is not about forcing yourself to be nice or pleasant in every situation, as if you are an actor taking on the role of a "nice person." You can be kind while telling someone a difficult truth. You can be kind while setting a firm boundary with someone. You can even be kind while in the presence of someone who has caused you suffering.

True kindness can take several forms: an unsolicited favor or a good deed, a moment of forgiveness, or an open heart and mind in a challenging situation. Buddhists refer to this type of true kindness by using the word *Maitri*. Maitri, also known as Metta, is a mindset consisting of benevolence, goodwill, and loving-kindness. This mindset is developed through the practice of being kind toward oneself and others.

As with generosity, kindness must be genuine. It stems from a place deep within you that truly wishes for all people to experience happiness and joy. You must also want this for yourself. In the words of Sharon Salzberg, a renowned Buddhist teacher, the nature of Maitri is to "reteach a thing its loveliness" (O'Brien, 2020). To practice Maitri, it is highly recommended that you begin within yourself. We all suffer from negative self-talk and insecurities, but we have the ability to show ourselves how valuable we really are. Once you are able to show yourself the loving-kindness you deserve, you can help others see it within themselves.

Altruism

To live selflessly—that is, to live without being consumed by one's own self-interest—is to practice altruism. Buddhists believe that altruism is a skill that leads to a deep connection with others, even those you do not know personally. When you are altruistic, you put others' needs and well-being before your own. You work alongside the rest of humanity without wondering how you will come out on top as the best of the best.

Living with such selflessness implies that you care for your entire community's success more than you care for your own. Because of this, you become an integral part of the human collective, like a gear in a grand machine. The Dalai Lama wrote that "practicing altruism is the real source of compromise and cooperation" (The 14th Dalai Lama, 2020). It means you are willing to put aside your self-interest in order to solve problems for the greater good. This may lead you to surrender your own beliefs or constitutions in order to compromise and create a better human experience for all.

Altruism can be extremely challenging to master, especially in modern times. There are billions of people in the world right now, many of whom have contrasting political and societal systems. Many times, the people within these opposing systems believe their system is superior to others. This results in disagreements, secessions, and wars, all rooted in severe self-interest. Yet, it is important to remember that all human beings are equal, despite their differing lifestyles. The Buddha taught his students that every person is a part of the human collective and no one is greater than another. When you can open your mind to this idea and accept it as truth, you will then be able to practice altruism and spread it to others.

Empathy

Empathy is the ability to understand someone's feelings so much so that you can feel them yourself. By empathizing with someone, you are recognizing their feelings as feelings you have also had. Sometimes, this means mentally putting yourself back in that moment to connect with the emotional experience you are sharing with another person. Other times, you can empathize with someone without having to consciously remember what it was like for you. Either way, you are sharing sentiments with another person and establishing a deeper connection with them.

A good example of empathy would be a time when you have comforted someone who was grieving. If this has happened in your life, you may remember feeling like you were also grieving, even if the circumstance had nothing to do with you directly. Perhaps you cried alongside the other person, letting them know they are not alone in their pain.

A more cheerful example would be when you celebrated with someone over one of their greatest accomplishments. For instance, maybe you had a close friend who was eagerly trying to conceive a child and start her family. When the day finally came that she found out she was pregnant, you shared her excitement and relief, celebrating even though it was not your accomplishment. This is empathy.

Empathy helps us develop deeper emotional connections with others, something that is highly valued within Buddhism. When you can empathize with the people around you, you become less self-involved and more a part of the human collective.

Compassion

Empathy leads us to have compassion for others, as well. Compassion is one of the most important parts of Buddhism, as it encourages us to act for the sake of others' well-being rather than just for our own. When you show someone compassion, you are acknowledging that you see them as an equal. With compassion, there is no room to feel better than anyone else. You simply want to see others being cared for because they deserve it.

Because compassion is such a significant component of Buddhism and therefore plays a major role in finding inner peace, it has been expanded on in the fourth chapter of this book. There are so many aspects of compassion through a Buddhist lens that it requires a more in-depth explanation.

Whether you were raised among adversity or luxury, it does not matter. You can nurture these skills at any point in your life, despite any circumstance you have faced. The poorest person can achieve the same inner peace as the richest person. The most famous person can achieve the same joyfulness as the most unknown person. Think of the Buddha, growing up with everything one could ever desire, only to abandon it all in the pursuit of deeper meaning. What matters is that you live with a pure mind, free from attachment and self-involvement.

Everyone has the ability to cultivate these emotional skills. Some folks are taught at a very young age to be kind and treat all people well, while others learn it as they grow older and become more aware. Some people develop their own sense of altruism on their own, while others have to be convinced. Although everyone grows at their own pace, both physically and emotionally, all human beings have the capacity to live with generosity, kindness, altruism, empathy, and compassion.

The Importance of Community

The emotional skills taught by the Buddha all share similarities. Not only do they each touch on a portion of the Eightfold Path, but they also focus on maintaining meaningful connections with others. Being part of a community is a necessary aspect of living a joyful life. In *The Book of Joy*, the Dalai Lama speaks on the social nature of human beings. Speaking to the book's author and Archbishop Desmond Tutu, the Dalai Lama says that human beings need love and friendships to survive. Without these connections, we would feel disconnected and alone for our entire lives, which would certainly inhibit our ability to feel joy.

Even the Buddha, when he began his years-long spiritual journey, benefitted from human connection. Though he often isolated himself from the outside world, he developed meaningful relationships with his teachers and spiritual guides. He found a community within the monasteries he visited and used his understanding of humanity to fuel his awakening. When he finally knew what it meant to reach nirvana, he began teaching others the path to enlightenment, wanting them to relish in the same fulfillment and joy.

What does your community look like? Do you have deep, important connections with others that fill your heart with meaning? If so, think about how those relationships have benefitted you and how they can continue to benefit you as you practice the skills leading to true joy. Ask yourself how you have acted with generosity toward others. Make a mental list of all the ways you have shown yourself the same generosity, the same loving-kindness.

If you struggle to answer those questions or to make such a list, think about the people you currently surround yourself with. Are you able to go to them when you need guidance? Are they able to come to you when they need a helping hand? In your life right now, who are the people you are genuinely happy to be around?

You may find that there are few people that fill these roles, and that is okay. It can be daunting to establish your community, especially as you get older, but it is worth the effort. Challenge yourself to reach out to others and show them unsolicited generosity and kindness. Connect with new people you have just met and learn their stories. Practice empathy by listening to them speak and recognizing the feelings behind their words. Spend time helping those who are unable to help themselves however you can.

Most importantly, live with good intentions and a pure mind. Try not to act out of hatred or anger. When those emotions do arise, acknowledge them for what they are and make room for positive thoughts. In time, they will come. By living this way, you will become part of the human collective, which will open so many doors for you to find your joy.

Exercises for Joyfulness

There are several practices and exercises that can help you achieve and maintain joyfulness. From meditations to physical tasks, at least one of the following techniques may be useful to you. Each one can be practiced as often or as infrequently as you please, though the more you practice them, the easier and more natural they will feel to you.

Mindfulness Practices

"Mindfulness is the energy that helps us recognize the conditions of happiness that are already present in our lives…" Thich Nhat Hanh once wrote. "When you breathe in, and you are aware of your in-breath, you touch the miracle of being alive" (Thich, 2023b). Through the act of slowing down and taking time to turn your focus inward, you tune into what it means to be alive, right here, right now. Being mindful, as you have learned, depends on your ability to release your thoughts of the past and future, remaining focused on the present moment.

Meditation is a tried and true method for practicing mindfulness, and all you need to do it is a safe place and your own willingness. Find a time during your day that allows you a few minutes of uninterrupted silence, if you can. This may be in your bedroom right after you wake up, before your children are calling for you, or you have to begin your work day. It may also be in the final moments of your day when everyone in your house is finally asleep and you have some time to yourself. Though you may feel tired from your long day of responsibilities, taking as little as five minutes to meditate can give you a deep sense of peace that will open your heart to joy.

When you're in your safe, quiet space, settle yourself into a comfortable position. It is typically recommended to sit while you meditate, but if you need to lie down, you may do so. Just try to stay awake enough to focus on your breathing. Once in position, take a few starting breaths to clear your mind. Breathe in and out slowly, feeling each intake of air deep within your core. Imagine the air filling your lungs and supplying your body with exactly what it wants. For many people, these first few breaths will be the deepest ones they have taken all day, maybe even all week. Follow each breath with your awareness. You may even think to yourself *I am breathing in, I am breathing out,* or whatever variation of the thought sits well with you. Acknowledge the energy you are giving to your body as you fill it with air. This is what is keeping you alive. This is what is allowing you to make beautiful changes in your life.

As you breathe, turn your focus to your body. Feel the places where it connects with the ground beneath you. If you are in a sitting position, feel how your hips, legs, and feet are pressing into the floor. You do not need to add any extra pressure; simply feel how your body holds you in position. If you are lying down, concentrate on the connection your entire body is making on the bed or floor.

You may feel certain areas of tension in your body. Perhaps you have been stressed and are holding it on your shoulders and neck, as many people do. Focus on this tension and breathe into it, telling yourself that you are releasing the stress in that area. Continue this type of mental release in all areas of your body that are harboring tension. Keep breathing in and out, slowly and naturally. By becoming aware of both your body and your breathing at the same time, you will develop a harmony that will, in turn, develop your ability to be mindful. It is a wonderful cycle for you to experience.

Remember, if outside thoughts enter your mind, do not try to shoo them away. Allow them to exist by giving them the moment of your attention that they desire, and then refocus on your breathing. Repeat these phrases in your thoughts: *I am breathing in, I am breathing out. I am releasing tension as I breathe.*

Walking Meditation

Thich Nhat Hahn also taught that you can practice this mind-body mindfulness while walking. You have most likely taken a casual stroll before, and walking meditation is no different. Find time in your day to take yourself on a walk around your neighborhood, city, or simply around your house. You do not need to make any extra effort while you do this. Just walk and breathe. Your thoughts may wander as you see and hear things around you that pique your interest. Let your thoughts go where they want.

Walk with the intention to practice mindfulness, to become more in tune with your body and the present moment. Do not set any other goals for yourself during your walking meditation, such as a specific distance or speed. This is not a test to see how fast you are or how much walking you can endure. It is purely a time for you to peacefully connect your mind and body.

Belly Breathing

Sometimes, although your intentions to practice mindfulness are pure, it can be challenging to release pent-up energy and restlessness. If you are someone who lives with an attention deficit disorder, it can feel impossible. One technique to combat this that Buddhist teachers show their students is called "belly breathing." Belly breathing is a method of breath control that is simple but effective in decreasing restlessness in the body.

Tsoknyi Rinpoche, a Tibetan Buddhist teacher, teaches the basics of belly breathing in a podcast called *Richer, Wiser, Happier* (Rinpoche, 2022). Essentially, the breathing technique is a way of using the energy stored in the mind and bringing it into your core through deep breathing. Tsoknyi Rinpoche tells listeners to breathe deeply, as they would in any meditative practice, and let that breath fill their bellies. It can help to imagine your core as a balloon. When you breathe in for a few seconds and focus that breath on your stomach, you fill up the balloon. Once the metaphorical balloon is full of air, you hold your breath for a few seconds. Of course, do not hold your breath so much that it becomes painful; just hold it enough to notice the shift in your energy from your head and neck to your belly.

Keep practicing this breath control method until you feel less restless and distracted. By doing this whenever it feels hard for you to focus on meditation, it will become more natural.

Tsoknyi Rinpoche's "Dropping" Technique

Many people struggle to focus on mindfulness because they are preoccupied with other thoughts.

Did I pay that important bill on time?

Are my kids going to eat the vegetables I packed in their lunch or just the sweet stuff?

What time was I supposed to finish meditating and go back to work?

Having conflicting thoughts is incredibly common, especially in today's day and age. All day, every day, we receive information from outside sources. Our phones send us constant notifications, televisions are turned on in almost every location, and our workplaces are often filled with gossip and stress. It is no wonder that our brains have become used to thinking about ten things at once without reprieve. It has become as natural to us as breathing.

What is not natural, though, is the power these outside influences have over our well-being. As far as historians know, this is the first time in human history that a person can download information from any part of the world in less than five seconds, all on a piece of technology the size of one's hand. This development has happened quickly and has taken our society by storm. While our ability to connect on a surface level has increased, our ability to ignore what is going on around us and focus inward has decreased. That is why mindfulness is a skill that needs to be practiced and developed over time.

So, if you are struggling to focus on your mindfulness practice and you have tried belly breathing, try another technique. In the same podcast interview mentioned above, Tsoknyi Rinpoche teaches listeners about a practice called "dropping meditation." He explains it as three things coming together: a gesture, an attitude in the mind, and a breath.

First, the gesture. You begin with your hands raised near eye level. Keep your fingers and wrists relaxed. It may feel odd, but that's okay. Then, lower your hands quickly, as if you are brushing invisible dust off of your shirt. It is a quick gesture and your hands should end in your lap or by your sides, depending on the position in which you have chosen to meditate.

While you perform the gesture of dropping your hands, think of the phrase *whatever happens, happens, and whatever doesn't happen, doesn't matter.* You may even say the phrase out loud as a mantra if you prefer. This is the attitude needed for a dropping meditation.

Finally, now that you know the gesture and attitude, combine them with your breathing. Breathe in as you normally would, raising your hands. Keep the *whatever happens* attitude in mind, or repeat the phrase and drop your hands down swiftly. The combination of these actions symbolizes the release of your worries and preoccupations. You are dropping them from your mind just as you are dropping your hands. This technique can be practiced on its own or as part of a longer meditation or mindfulness practice.

Setting Intentions

The Buddha emphasized the idea that there are four main sources of happiness: edible food, sense impressions, consciousness, and intentions (Weber, 2020). The latter plays a large role in a person's day-to-day happiness. To live with deep awareness and inner peace helps to set intentions for each day.

Douglas Abrams, the author of *The Book of Joy* featuring the Dalai Lama, gives readers an inside look at how setting intentions can benefit their well-being. Essentially, intention-setting is when a person makes goals for how they will approach the day. The reason it is not simply called "goal-setting" is because intentions usually hold a much deeper, more spiritual essence. For example, a Buddhist nun may wake up in the morning and set an intention to treat all those she interacts with during the day with kindness and compassion. It is an intention of attitude rather than a tangible accomplishment. That being said, intentions can be combined with actionable goals to fulfill both the spiritual and physical parts of oneself. In this way, an intention to be compassionate can be accompanied by the goal of expressing gratitude to at least one person that day.

To practice setting your own intentions, Douglas Abrams recommends starting in the morning. If you already have a meditation practice in the morning, intention-setting is a perfect addition. Begin by meditating as you normally would, by sitting comfortably and breathing into every part of your body to release tension. Then, look within yourself and identify your heart's desire. What do you wish for the people in your life, including yourself? This can be overall happiness, a feeling of gratitude, the ability to forgive others, or anything else. It may help you to think back on what you know about the Buddha and his intentions for the world during his spiritual journey.

When you have identified what it is your heart wants for your community, you can begin to set your intentions for the day. Abrams includes examples like showing everyone you meet during the day loving kindness, as well as practicing patience with your family and children. These are just examples, however. Your intentions can be anything that you feel you can commit to that day. If you are feeling troubled by someone's past actions toward you, a helpful intention may be to focus on forgiveness.

Your intentions can be kept as internal thoughts or you can write them down in a journal. For many people, having a written intention can serve as a reminder to remain mindful throughout the day.

In the event that you cannot come up with your own specific intentions, you may consider using what Abrams describes as an adapted version of the Tibetan Four Immeasurables, an ancient Buddhist prayer. The prayer is:

May all beings attain happiness.

May all beings be free from suffering.

May all beings never be separated from joy.

May all beings abide in equanimity.

Chapter 3:

Living Freely

The Notion of Free Will

What does freedom mean to you? Is it the ability to make your own choices, or perhaps, a feeling you get when you practice independence? For some, freedom may be as simple as speaking one's mind without fear of admonishment or punishment. It is as subjective as any word could possibly be, and its meaning is different for everyone. In the dictionary, *freedom* does not even have one single definition. The term is defined as a political right, a liberation from slavery or powerful restraint, and even "the quality of being outspoken" (Merriam-Webster, 2023). Clearly, there is no universal meaning behind the word.

Despite this, *freedom* is mentioned in countless government documents, declarations, religious texts, and more. For instance, the United Nations Universal Declaration of Human Rights mentions the word over 20 times, referencing the privileges and abilities held by human beings (United Nations, 1948). It is a term that upholds the entire meaning of the document. In this declaration, freedom is often associated with the idea that human beings have free will, meaning their decisions are theirs alone and cannot be made by anyone—or anything—else.

While the notion of free will in this context is one based on ethics and independence, the Buddha had a contrasting idea. Though he believed in the humane treatment and equality of all people, regardless of their identity or social status, he did not fully agree that everyone had free will. The Buddha, as you now know, believed in karma. He taught his followers that their actions in the past and present have consequences in the present and future. The idea that a person can determine every aspect of their own life as they please does not align with the beliefs of Buddhists.

Because of karma, a person *does* have the ability to change the course of their life. That is to say, the benevolent choices they make can bring them good fortune and, ultimately, enlightenment. Similarly, the harmful choices they make can bring them farther from nirvana, filling their life path with misfortune and more suffering. In this way, a person has the ability to choose the course of their life. However, they are making choices that are dependent on karmic belief, not on their own free will.

Scholars and practitioners of Buddhism have long argued about these ideas. There are various articles and debates online that question the amount of free will human beings truly have, if they have any at all. There are also scientists who have joined in on the conversation, combining their research with the ideals and beliefs of Buddhists. In one article, a Buddhist monk worked alongside a neuroscientist to discuss the connection between the ancient philosophy and biological science. The two men determined that the idea of "free will" is a manmade illusion created by societal norms and beliefs. On the neuroscientific side of the discussion, it is believed that the human brain is made up of complex functions that determine a person's decision-making.

Dieter Jaeger, the neuroscientist involved in writing the article, explains that all decisions and behaviors are dictated by the state of the brain, meaning "human behavior and decision-making will remain unpredictable at the level of individual decisions" (Jaeger & Gonpo, 2021). Essentially, a person can only make decisions based on how their brain is functioning in the moment. The mind's ability to choose is not based on free will but rather a series of neurological events.

Lobsang Gonpo, the monk who wrote the article alongside Dieter Jaeger, provided insight into Buddhist beliefs of the *self*. Gonpo writes that, through a Buddhist lens, all decisions and behaviors are relative. That is, every human experience is interdependent and reliant on outside causes. In the same way that a person's actions can determine what happens in their current and future lives, a person's actions are determined by what happens before them. Everything that happens is based on cause and effect. Therefore, no decisions are made based on true freedom of will.

What Jaeger and Gonpo conclude in their article is the idea that free will is a man-made idea, not a true phenomenon or aspect of the human experience. This does not mean that a person cannot make decisions in their life because of a predetermined destiny. Instead, it simply means that the moments leading up to a person's choices have just as much control over the outcome as the choices themselves.

You may be wondering how this conclusion ties into your own life. Whether you believe in karma, total free will, or a combination of both, you can benefit from the knowledge that your actions have consequences that can change your life. The good that you put out into the world can come back to benefit you, and the negativity you put out can amplify the suffering you feel. If you take the time to focus on being compassionate, kind, and generous, you open yourself up to more joy in your life. For those that believe in karma, this is the best way to ensure a future life with less suffering.

Mental Freedom

The Buddha did not limit his beliefs to the argument of free will versus karma. The spiritual teacher also taught his students about mental freedom. The idea of freedom is commonly associated with a lack of physical restriction, such as one's freedom to speak or act without punishment. What many people do not realize, though, is that freedom extends past physical actions.

Through Buddhist practices, a person will come to understand that there are many mental and emotional restrictions that must be overcome. As the previous chapters explain, unwavering attachment leads to suffering. When you are attached to a certain outcome or idea, rather than accepting whatever happens, you are met with negative emotions. In this way, your mental freedom is restricted by your attachments. To be genuinely free, you must liberate yourself from your desperate desires, especially those that are rooted in anger, greed, and fear. The mind can become a prisoner to such negative emotions, leaving it unable to experience peace, the true source of freedom.

For the Buddha, the highest level of mental freedom existed only in nirvana. With every lesson the Buddha learned, he made steps toward his own enlightenment and mental liberation. Even if your goal is not as lofty as the Buddha's, you can achieve your own mental freedom by seeking inner peace.

The Wisdom of Thich Nhat Hanh

Thich Nhat Hanh once said that freedom is not something that can be given or granted to you; you must cultivate it yourself. No matter how independent or unrestrained you are in your physical life, true freedom can only come from the work you do for yourself to achieve inner peace. Mental freedom will bring you more liberation than any other kind.

Before Thich Nhat Hanh died, he had a distinct philosophy for his students. Because one must cultivate their own mental freedom, it is necessary to do so in every waking moment. When you arise with a new day, you can choose to be free. With each breath you take, you can do so with a free mind. Thich Nhat Hanh told his students: "When you eat, eat as a free person. When you walk, walk as a free person. When you breathe, breathe as a free person" (Thich, 2023a). Cultivate your freedom by acknowledging that you are not bound by the negative thoughts in your mind. You are not a slave to the worries, disappointments, or fears inside of you. When you recognize this as truth, you can live each day as a free person.

The renowned Buddhist monk declared his own personal, mental freedom by rejoicing in the miracle of life. He spoke joyfully on the fact that every day he woke up alive, he was given the freedom to live one more day.

Exercises for Freedom

Practice Authenticity

Attachment is heavily influenced by expectations. When you expect a certain outcome, for example, you attach your emotional state to that expectation. If the expected outcome does not happen, the attachment you felt to it may transform into anger or frustration. This can also occur when you take on the expectations of others, especially those whose opinions are important to you.

As children, many girls are encouraged to have big dreams and believe in themselves. They are often told that they are capable of anything they put their minds to. Yet, when these girls enter womanhood, what once was encouragement from others becomes doubt. The women that were originally told that they could do anything are introduced to a society that was built to challenge them in every possible way. On one side, some believe women can never live up to the successes of men. On another side comes the order to do what men do and do it better, proving the patriarchy wrong. Then, there are those who demand that women choose between creating a family or being successful in their careers, doubting that both paths can be balanced together.

Finally, there is the side of the young women in question, who simply want to do what makes them happy. For so many of these women, the pressure to not only achieve but exceed societal expectations outweighs the importance of being authentic to themselves. They choose to live their lives for other people, whether that means being the primary caregiver of their growing family, working tirelessly to prove their abilities, or both. Little to no action is made to produce a lifestyle that promotes authenticity and inner peace, mainly because there is simply no time left in the day to focus on such a task.

Thus, women become attached to the outstanding expectations thrust upon them. Be a caring, involved mother, but also be able to make a living to show that you are not succumbing to traditional, patriarchal values. Be strong and demand the best for yourself, but do not come across too bossy or domineering. Spend quality time with your partner to encourage a happy life together, but do not be so absorbed by your relationship that you cannot spend time with others. Be someone who can balance everything without feeling overwhelmed.

It is nearly impossible to live up to these expectations. As a human being, you are destined to lack in some areas while thriving in others. Trying to achieve everything that is expected of you while ignoring what feels genuine and authentic to your identity will only restrict you from finding joy. Your attachment to these expectations, and subsequent disappointment in not achieving them all, will keep you from finally liberating your mind.

To release yourself from the mental bondage of the world's expectations, you must follow your own path. It is imperative that you understand what feels right for yourself and go after it. Ask yourself what it means to be authentically *you*: Who would your authentic self surround herself with; what lifestyle would she most want to live; how would she navigate difficult situations? The answers you find to these questions will take you one step closer to freeing your mind and finding peace.

Think Before Speaking and Acting

Mindfulness is a significant contributor to mental freedom. First and foremost, understanding the point of mental freedom is a mindfulness practice on its own. By learning what it means to free your mind, you are practicing looking inward at your own thought processes and emotions. You are becoming mindful of the restrictions that are put in place by certain ideas. Additionally, mindfulness in relation to mental freedom can be practiced by thinking before you speak or act.

This is not the same "think before you speak" admonishment you may have heard as a child after saying something out of turn. Rather, it is a phrase you may remind yourself of when you are overcome with negative emotions. Although it is common for people to speak harshly or out of anger when their emotions are running rampant, it is something that the Buddha believes should be avoided. Your negative emotions play an important role in your ability to acknowledge suffering and practice compassion, but they can also cause you to behave without first recognizing the consequences of your words or actions.

How many times have you said something that you regretted or that hurt someone deeply? Out of these times, how often did speaking out of negative emotions make you feel worse instead of better? Thinking back on these moments, consider how the situation could have turned out if you had taken a moment to think about your words before you spoke them aloud. Perhaps, given the chance, you would have chosen not to indulge in your anger, frustration, fear, or disappointment. This may have allowed a more positive experience, one filled with spiritual growth and mindfulness rather than regret and guilt.

By remaining mindful of your thoughts before they are spoken, you are performing two components of the Eightfold Path: Right Mindfulness and Right Speech. Taking a moment to consider your negative emotions before voicing them plays into Right Mindfulness, while choosing to instead speak without anger, hatred, or harm plays into Right Speech. The two components go hand-in-hand to create a benevolent and compassionate mindset.

The practice of thinking before you speak is straightforward, though it is not easy. It takes patience toward yourself and others to refrain from saying the first negative thing that comes to mind. Because the brain craves instant gratification, as you learned in the previous chapter, it can lead you to believe that speaking out of negativity is the fastest way to relieve your inner frustrations. For a moment, it can feel as though you have released your negativity once and for all. This moment is fleeting, however, and not a genuine instance of mental freedom.

In heated moments, you must train yourself to ignore the desire for instant gratification and focus on pausing before speaking. It will take practice, as with all Buddhist teachings, but you will develop the skill with time. When you feel negative and are eager to release your emotions through your words, take a deep breath. Consider what it would mean to speak these thoughts out loud. Then, consider the empowerment you may feel after choosing to speak with kindness and generosity instead. Right Speech means being honest about your feelings without putting harmful emotions into the world around you.

It may also help to remind yourself of the Buddha's now-famous quote: "What you think, you become" (Parachin, 2023). Reframe the negativity in your mind and replace it with understanding and compassion for yourself and others.

Freedom In Every Smile

Plum Village, a Buddhist monastery and community established with the help of Thich Nhat Hanh, has an ongoing annual tradition that encourages its founder's philosophy on mental freedom. Thanks to the online resources provided by Plum Village, this tradition has now been introduced and encouraged in a more widespread manner.

The tradition is the offering of two parallel verses to mark the Lunar New Year, a cultural milestone achieved on the first new moon of the Lunar calendar. The community members of the Plum Village monastery celebrate the Lunar New Year by writing two Buddhist verses and displaying them in a community space. The verses are:

> *Peace in every step. Freedom in every smile.*

These phrases are written on individual pieces of paper cut into diamond shapes. The verses, also known as a couplet, serve as a reminder to seek peace for yourself and others and to find freedom through joyfulness.

To take part in this simple practice, you can cut two pieces of paper into diamonds and write the first verse on one and the second verse on the other. Then, all you need to do is display the verses somewhere you will frequently see them, such as on a wall near a light switch or by your bathroom mirror. You may also write the couplet on a regular piece of paper, a whiteboard, or even a sticky note. The physical appearance of the words does not matter nearly as much as the meaning they hold. As long as they remind you to seek peace and mental freedom, they are doing their job.

Chapter 4:

Acting With Compassion

A constant fixture throughout Buddhist philosophy is compassion. It is an aspect of Buddhism that exists in every lesson taught and learned. The Westernized view of compassion is that it is merely an emotion with which many people are in tune. From a Buddhist perspective, however, compassion is so much more. Not only is it an emotion, but it is also a state of mind, skill, and aspiration for Buddhist practitioners. For one to identify as a student of Buddhism, one must identify with compassion.

For the Buddha, compassion was the key that opened the door to enlightenment. To have compassion in the eyes of the Buddha, one must treat all human beings as their equals, deserving of loving-kindness and empathy. Most importantly, compassion is the aspiration for all people to be free from suffering, despite knowing that suffering is inevitable. In simpler terms, the Buddhist idea of compassion is that it is an expression of hope for all.

It is also believed by many that compassion is a natural human experience. In the same article that was introduced in Chapter 3, written by a neuroscientist and Buddhist monk, compassion was proven to be an innate feature of human brains, as well as the brains of other mammals (Jaeger & Gonpo, 2021). Both Buddhist practitioners and biological scientists agree that compassion is something that comes naturally to human beings. It is an intuitive instinct rather than a skill developed solely through practice. When you act compassionately, you are acting in accordance with your natural abilities. It should not feel too difficult or like a major sacrifice.

There is a Sanskrit often used in Buddhist teachings that encapsulates this notion of acting compassionately, called *karuna*. Karuna is a practice that is deeply important to those who are working towards enlightenment. The meaning of the word is "any action taken to diminish the suffering of others" (Reiki Administrator, 2015). When one develops Karuna within themselves, they are harnessing the power of compassionate action.

Compassion can be acted upon in various ways. You may show compassion to others by supporting them during times of distress or pain. You may show compassion to yourself by releasing any feelings of guilt or shame for actions you have taken in the past. You may even show compassion to all of humanity by hoping for collective peace and joyfulness.

The Components of Compassion

Because compassion holds so many meanings and definitions, it can be helpful for learners to understand it as an overarching theme that covers multiple components. Within compassion are individual mindsets and attitudes, all with distinct significance. To be compassionate or to develop Karuna, one should become familiar with activating four different states of mind: solidarity, forgiveness, gratitude, and self-compassion.

Solidarity

The first step of any compassionate action is to view all human beings as equal to yourself. Though there may be people that have wronged you or made you feel like a lesser being, you must view them as your equal counterparts rather than your opposition. Understand that there are no "better" humans, nor are there "worse" humans. Everyone is equal to one another, regardless of actions they have taken or behaviors they have exhibited.

You may believe that there are villains in the world, those who are filled with evil and do not deserve the happiness that comes from enlightenment. Perhaps you believe some people deserve more happiness than others, for whatever reason. To truly be compassionate, you must release these beliefs once and for all. There are certainly people who have caused immense harm to others, but you must remember that these people have also experienced suffering. There is not a single person who is unfamiliar with pain and misfortune in some way or another. No one's suffering is worse or better than anyone else's. Despite the harm some people have caused, understand that they are your equal. They are human, just like you.

Once you come to terms with this idea, which can take quite a long time, you will be able to understand what it means to live in solidarity with all of humanity. Human beings are part of a collective existence. Buddhist philosophy determines that there is no true individual self. You may be an independent person, meaning you are one body and one soul, but you are intertwined with every other person on this Earth. You are not so different from others that you exist in a unique realm. You are one part of a whole. This connection is what Buddhist teachers call *interdependence.*

Think of interdependence in relation to the food you eat. When you take a bite of an apple, consider the path it took to get to your mouth. Maybe you purchased the apple from the grocery store. Maybe the grocery store purchased their apple stock from a farm far away. Maybe the farmer purchased the apple seeds from someone else. Now, taking a simple bite from an apple becomes an exercise in human interdependence. You are benefitting from the work put in by countless other people, most of whom you may not have and never will cross physical paths with. Yet, you are still connected through each other's actions.

Now, take your understanding of interdependence and apply it to every aspect of your life. Imagine the ground you walk on to be the same ground that hundreds, maybe thousands, of others have walked on before you. Think of the people that will walk the same ground years in the future. When you feel emotions, whether they are pleasurable or difficult, think of all the other human beings in the world feeling the same emotions. They very well may be feeling what you are feeling at the same moment, thousands of miles away from you. The pain you feel in times of suffering is the same pain someone else has felt or will one day feel, even if the causes of the pain are different. This is what it means to practice solidarity. This is compassionate action.

Forgiveness

The second component of compassion is forgiveness. You most likely have a basic knowledge of forgiveness, but do you truly understand what the act of forgiving someone can do for your spirit? For many Buddhists, forgiveness allows one to release the burden of resentment or attachment to the desire for a different past. When this burden is released, your mind and heart make room for enlightenment.

The act of forgiveness extends farther than the traditional belief that when someone gives you an apology, you tell them it is all water under the bridge. In reality, forgiveness can be offered even when no apology is given. It is not an act of reciprocity in that forgiveness must be acknowledged by all who are involved. You can forgive someone for their wrongdoings without them knowing they are being forgiven. While it can make the other person or people feel happier knowing they are forgiven, your forgiveness is for your own sake. You must seek forgiveness for no reason other than to lessen the emotional burden in your mind.

When you do not practice forgiveness, you allow the anger and resentment inside of you to rise to unmanageable levels. You become consumed with the idea that remaining angry is more important than purifying the mind. By living with this attitude, you are doing yourself a disservice. There is a well-known saying that goes something like this: *Holding resentment in your heart is like drinking poison and waiting for others to die.* If you are withholding forgiveness in the hope that the person who has wronged you will suffer, you are only creating more suffering for yourself. When you forgive, you get to reap the benefits of living with compassion.

Gratitude

The third component of compassion is the expression of gratitude. This entails acknowledging when something has served you well and being thankful for it. Gratitude also means being grateful for what you have not had to suffer, such as illness or misfortune. In some ways, you can even be grateful for things that initially appear negative. In *The Book of Joy*, the author points out that Buddhist philosophy allows one to be grateful for those that have done nothing but harm to them. These people, who one may consider enemies, are also considered the "most precious spiritual teachers" because they reveal lessons that may not have emerged without adversity (Lama et al., 2016).

True gratitude can be expressed for anything that brings you enlightenment or joy. It is important to recognize what has existed in your life in this way. You may be grateful for your family and their health, your well-being, or the food you eat every day. You may even be grateful to just live another day. By expressing gratitude, be it aloud or in your mind, you are encouraging positivity within yourself. Gratitude can also help you turn a painful situation into a learning experience. When you are injured, you can offer your gratitude for the ability to feel pain because it means you are alive. When someone breaks your heart, you can still offer gratitude for the pain because it means that you experienced true love.

You may even express gratitude for things that did not happen to you. Maybe you had an experience that could have ended much more negatively than it really had. Practice gratitude by being thankful for the lesser suffering. Perhaps you lived an entire day free from suffering. Try offering gratitude for the length of time you were given to feel every emotion other than pain. Your deepest compassion can come from your ability to be grateful for what is happening to you right now.

Self-Compassion

The final component of compassion is the practice of being compassionate towards yourself. This means forgiving yourself for any wrongdoings you may have done in the past, expressing gratitude for your resilience and self-work, and allowing yourself to connect deeply with others. Self-compassion is often more difficult to practice than compassion toward others, mainly because it requires self-awareness and introspection.

It can be difficult to look inward and observe the true nature of your being. However, one cannot truly develop Karuna without exercising self-compassion. No matter how many people you support or empathize with, your ability to act compassionately will only be in full force when you can do it for yourself. If you are struggling with the memory of a mistake you once made, treat yourself as you would anyone else by offering forgiveness. Remind yourself that holding a grudge will only make you feel worse.

If you experience a moment of self-judgment or negative self-talk, take a deep breath and move forward with an open heart. You are a human being that is bound to make mistakes and learn from them. You are flawed, just like everyone else. Give yourself the compassion you would give to your best friend or your sister, someone you value highly.

Exercises for Compassion

Gratitude Practice

A simple but effective practice for gratitude is writing down what you are grateful for. For some people, this practice is best performed through journaling, in which they can look back and remind themselves what they were grateful for in the past, as well as write down what they are grateful for in the present. Others prefer a clean slate for expressing gratitude and will choose to write what they are grateful for on an individual piece of paper.

You may choose the method that works best for you. The point of the practice is to turn your thoughts of gratitude into physical, visual representations. Similarly to speaking your gratitude out loud, writing it down releases it from your mind into the world.

The following are some examples of what you may choose to write, or you can come up with your own:

- I am grateful for my physical and mental well-being.
- I am grateful for the well-being of my loved ones.
- I am grateful to be alive today.
- I am grateful to live in a safe, secure home.
- I am grateful to have the ability to express myself authentically.

- I am grateful for my emotions.

- I am grateful for the lessons I have learned through my suffering.

- I am grateful for the chance to alleviate the suffering of others.

- I am grateful for myself and my willingness to learn.

No matter what you choose to write down, do so with an open mind and heart. Be aware of the intention with which you are writing. This is not a practice that should be done out of obligation or necessity. It is simply a way for you to acknowledge all that you have to be thankful for in the present moment.

Forgiveness Practice

To meditate on forgiveness, you must be open to feeling any difficult emotions that arise. Forgiveness meditation can be a powerful and transformative experience, especially for anyone who is struggling with feelings of hatred, resentment, or guilt. For this meditation, find a comfortable position and tune into your breathing, as you would with any other meditation.

Once you have taken some deep, clarifying breaths, begin to think about someone or something you are holding negativity towards. Take a moment to remember how you were hurt in the situation, but try not to let your mind run wild with blame and a subjective narrative. All you should think about is what happened, how it made you feel, and why you must release the burden of those feelings.

Now, open yourself up to the notion of forgiveness. It may help to repeat the word in your mind or out loud a few times to get comfortable with it. When you are ready, repeat the following phrases:

- I forgive you for the harm you caused.
- I am offering you forgiveness and releasing the burden of negativity.

Pause for a moment and sit with the feelings that emerge, or acknowledge a lack of feeling. Take another deep breath and release any tension you feel throughout your body. Repeat these steps as many times as you feel is necessary.

Next, consider a time when you felt disappointed in yourself or ashamed because of something you said or did. Again, remember how it felt and why you feel it is necessary to unburden yourself, but do not get caught up in the details of the event. When you are ready, repeat the following phrases:

- I forgive myself for the harm I caused.
- I forgive myself for the mistakes I have made.
- I am offering myself forgiveness and releasing the burden of negativity.

If you feel that you have caused harm to someone else, you may also repeat the phrase:

- I am asking for forgiveness for the harm I caused.

Just like before, take a moment to exist alongside your emotions. When forgiving yourself or asking for forgiveness, you may be overcome with unexpected emotions. Do not push the feelings away. Let those feelings spend time in your mind without being judged or punished. If necessary, repeat these steps.

Karuna Meditation

A Karuna, or compassion, meditation focuses on offering prayers to oneself and others. Begin this practice as you would any other meditation, in a comfortable seated or lying position in a peaceful environment. Remove any possible distractions that surround you, such as your cell phone, and try to be in a place that has limited outside noise. To feel the complete benefit of a Karuna meditation, you must be able to concentrate on your intentions without being distracted by what is going on around you.

When you are in a comfortable position, begin focusing on your breathing. When you practice enough meditation in your daily life, this beginning stage will become natural to you. Breathe deeply, in and out, and feel your abdomen rise and fall. You may also choose to place your hand on your chest or belly to connect you more closely with your body.

After you have become aware of your breath, imagine someone in your life who means very much to you. This can be a family member, alive or deceased, a loving pet, or a dear friend. Keep their image in your mind as you breathe and make space for whatever emotions or sensations arise within you. While doing this, think of the following phrases:

- May you be free from physical suffering.

- May you be free from mental suffering.

- May you be free from all suffering.

- May you live in peace.

By silently repeating these words, you are presenting your loved one with compassion. Let yourself relish the idea that the person or being that you love so much will experience true happiness and joy in their lifetime.

Now, think back to a time when this person or being experienced suffering, whether it was physical or emotional. Allow yourself to feel how they were feeling at that time. It may bring you sadness, worry, or heartache, and that is okay. Feel whatever comes up for you when thinking about your loved one.

Again, silently repeat the phrases above. When you finish, imagine all the pain and suffering felt by your loved one has lifted and rejoice in their freedom.

Next, imagine yourself in your mind. The image you see may be a younger version of yourself, the current version, or one that has yet to exist. Whatever version you see, hold their image in your mind and silently say the following phrases:

- May I be free from physical suffering.

- May I be free from mental suffering.

- May I be free from all suffering.

- May I live in peace.

If your hand is already placed over your heart, keep it there. If it is on your stomach or resting beside you, move your hand so that it is on your chest. Feel your heartbeat as you offer compassion to yourself. Continue breathing comfortably.

Finally, imagine all of the other human beings alive right now. Think about the circumstances they may have experienced in their lifetimes. They have felt all of the emotions you have felt. Hold them in your thoughts as you silently repeat the final phrases:

- May we all be free from physical suffering.
- May we all be free from mental suffering.
- May we all be free from all suffering.
- May we all live in peace.

As you complete this practice and return your focus to your breathing, remember to be gentle with yourself. Know that you have just sent compassion into the world for all to feel. Take a moment to sit with any emotions that arise.

Mani Mantra

There is also a mantra that Buddhists use to cultivate compassion, often called the Mani mantra or compassion mantra. In Sanskrit, the mantra is written as *Om Mani Padme Hum* and pronounced like "ohm-mah-nee-pahd-may-hum" (Morrison, 2020). Each word within the mantra has its own meaning in Sanskrit: Om, signifying the vibrational sound of the universe; Mani, meaning *jewel* and representing ethics and patience; Padme, meaning *lotus* and representing diligence and concentration; and Hum, the final syllable used to represent the wisdom and unity of the mantra.

When put together, Om Mani Padme Hum translates to *Praise to the Jewel in the Lotus*. This is a reference to the ancient image of the Bodhisattva Avalokiteshvara, the human embodiment of compassion in Buddhism, sitting in the center of a giant lotus flower.

The Mani mantra is meant to be chanted during meditation to cultivate compassion within oneself. To practice this tradition, all you have to do is sit comfortably in a meditative pose and repeat the phrase. You may do this silently or speak the words out loud. As you do, you can picture yourself sitting atop a lotus flower, like the Bodhisattva Avalokiteshvara, cultivating endless compassion.

According to yoga practitioners and those who frequently recite the Mani mantra, there are various benefits besides developing Karuna. For one, reciting the mantra can clear your mind and help you focus on the present moment. The vibrations of the mantra may also help release tension and judgment that is stuck in your body (Morrison, 2020).

Chapter 5:

Welcoming Difficult Emotions

Everyone experiences difficult emotions throughout their life. Anger, despair, guilt, frustration... the list goes on. From the earliest days of life to the last, difficult emotions exist. As a child, negative thoughts and feelings are solved through tears, tantrums, and consolation from adults. When a person grows older, they are taught to either process their emotions in a healthy way or push them aside with the hope that the feelings will disappear. Unfortunately, many people are more familiar with the latter. Not knowing how to deal with difficult emotions can result in devastating consequences, some of which can result in physical and mental harm.

Mental illnesses affect billions of people every day, preventing them from experiencing a full range of positive emotions and mindsets. Many people living with mental illness deal with complicated, overwhelming thought processes that make positive thinking exponentially more difficult. Conditions like depression and anxiety are much more challenging to overcome than ordinary negative thoughts because of their neurological and hormonal effects.

These conditions do not discriminate by gender, age, or social status. However, there are significant differences between women and men suffering from certain mental illnesses. As of right now, more women than men are dealing with anxiety and depression.

Anxiety diagnoses in women are two times more likely than diagnoses in men, and one in five women suffer from a mental disorder (Health Assured Team, 2023). These numbers are steadily increasing, as well. That is why learning to process emotions and deal with them in a healthy way is now more important than ever.

Difficult Emotions Serve a Purpose

The key to processing and overcoming difficult emotions lies in the understanding that each emotion exists for a reason. The Buddha emphasized the inevitability of suffering and the fact that all human beings experience pain during their lifetimes. There is not a single person who has lived a life free from negative emotions. Guilt, anger, grief, sadness, and disappointment reach everyone at some point in time. It can seem unthinkable to find a deeper meaning or purpose for these emotions, especially in the midst of feeling them, but it is not impossible. With every negative emotion you feel, you are learning a lesson about the nature of human existence.

Take grief, for example. When you experience the loss of someone or something that means the world to you, you will most likely grieve. This grief manifests as a deep sorrow within you, almost like a fog of devastation throughout your body. You feel grief in your heart, mind, and soul. The grief you feel is, in a way, a manifestation of the love you have cultivated during your life. You cannot mourn the loss of something you did not love, that you did not find happiness in. Your grief is a reminder that you are capable of feeling the most wonderful emotions human life has to offer, despite the knowledge that they will someday be met with sorrow. It can be overwhelmingly painful to grieve a loss, but that experience can be a great emotional tool. By allowing yourself to grieve, instead of forcing the pain away and pretending it does not exist, you are empowering yourself to become a more compassionate, vulnerable being.

Jack Kornfield, an American writer and Buddhist teacher, describes the process of grieving as a natural cycle, "like the spring after winter" (Kornfield, 2017). Though it may take a long time for grief to be outweighed by compassion and understanding, it does happen eventually, as long as you allow yourself to feel the pain and suffering without restriction. Let yourself cry through your grief. Make art or create written works about what you are mourning. Above all else, welcome all of your emotions as equal components of your existence in this life. Do not attach yourself to the idea that the difficult feelings inside of you are bad or unnecessary, as if they are parts of you that should not exist. Treat them with acceptance and understanding, and watch how your pain slowly transforms into compassion for yourself, continuing its natural, inevitable cycle.

Suffering Stems From Reactivity

It is easy to assume that the suffering one experiences is due to the difficult emotions one feels, but this is not exactly true. Yes, feelings like anger and sorrow are painful, though they are not the root of suffering. Difficult emotions are as necessary and unavoidable as pleasant emotions. It is one's reaction to difficult emotions that causes true pain and suffering.

When you experience moments of joy or excitement, your reaction is most likely a positive one. You probably want to relish those moments and make the pleasurable feelings last as long as possible. Contrarily, when you experience moments of grief or frustration, you might have a hostile reaction. Negative emotions do not feel as uplifting or beneficial as positive ones, so your initial reaction may be to push them away as soon as you can. Although it is understandable, this hostile reaction is unfair to the difficult emotions you are feeling. Every emotion inside of you is equal—there are no "bad" emotions or "good" emotions. They all serve their own distinct purpose. By reacting to difficult emotions with hatred and disdain, you are inhibiting your human experience, thus creating more suffering for yourself.

It is possible for you to treat your difficult emotions with the same openness and compassion as you would your pleasurable emotions. You have the capacity to react to all of your feelings with acceptance instead of pushing away the emotions that are more painful to experience. Once you learn to react fairly, you can greatly reduce emotional suffering.

Exercises for Diffusing Negativity

Breathing Exercises for Anxiety and Stress

Breath Awareness Meditation

A brief and straightforward technique for dealing with feelings like anxiety and stress is to practice a breath awareness meditation. It is similar to regular meditation in that it requires you to focus on your in-and-out breath, but it is slightly more advanced in the context of soothing anxiety. You can do this at the end of a stressful day or in the midst of feeling anxious.

Position yourself in a comfortable meditative pose, either lying down or sitting with a straight spine. Take a few deep breaths to clear your mind, focusing on every inhale and exhale. Allow your breathing to become slower and steadier while you feel the oxygen enter every part of your body. Thich Nhat Hanh recommends breathing deeply into the belly when you are experiencing stress and anxiety.

With each breath in, mentally repeat the phrases *I am not my stress* and *I am not my anxiety*. As you breathe out, tell yourself *I have survived my emotions before*. Continue this practice for at least one minute, allowing yourself to find truth in the mantras and comfort in your breathing.

If you have time, you may practice this for as long as you want, even up to an hour or two. Do not overwhelm yourself with a time limit, however. Simply breathe deeply and repeat the phrases in your mind until you feel that your anxiety and stress have subsided.

Box Breathing

Another popular breathing technique is called box breathing or square breathing. The practice is simple. While you are in a meditative position, even if you are just sitting at your desk or in the driver's seat of your parked car, close your eyes and take one deep breath.

Then, when you are in tune with your breathing, inhale for four seconds. Count the seconds in your mind slowly. When you reach the count of four, hold your breath for another four seconds. When you again reach the count of four, exhale for four more seconds. At the end of your exhale, breath normally for four seconds, and then repeat the practice.

It can help you to imagine each breath as one equal side of a square. As you breathe and count, imagine you are drawing a square in your mind. Complete this practice as many times as you need until your anxiety and stress have lessened.

Atlas of Emotions

With the spiritual guidance of the Dalai Lama, a psychology professor has developed a unique tool to help people better understand the science behind their emotions. Dr. Paul Ekman, who works for the University of California in San Francisco, created the Atlas of Emotions. The tool works as a timeline that identifies the process of human emotions as they turn into reactions and behaviors. According to Ekman, the Dalai Lama approached him with the idea that human beings deserved a physical map of their emotional states to reach inner peace, in the same way that explorers use maps to find their treasures (Razzetti, 2019). Both the Dalai Lama and Dr. Ekman knew the importance of understanding one's emotions through self-awareness, kickstarting their journey to create an easy-to-comprehend, interactive tool.

The Atlas of Emotions shows users their emotional processes from beginning to end, that is, from the conception of emotion to the behavior it ignites in a person. Not only does the tool explain the meanings of the five universal emotions—anger, enjoyment, fear, disgust, and sadness—but it also shows how these emotions can be triggered, escalated, and overcome.

Though the main purpose of the Atlas of Emotions is to help people become self-aware, it also teaches users how to take constructive action after an emotional trigger instead of destructive action. The Dalai Lama explains that constructive action happens when a person can meet their emotions with logic and reasoning, allowing them to process what they are feeling in a helpful way. When you are overcome with anger, for example, you may react by insulting someone, arguing with them, or using physical force. This is considered destructive because it causes harm to both yourself and the other person. A constructive action in response to anger would be to pause, sit with the emotion, and talk things through calmly.

The Atlas of Emotions is a powerful tool for better understanding your own emotional states, especially if you struggle to understand why you react in certain ways.

Grief Meditation

Buddhist practitioner, Jack Kornfield, has published a meditation to guide others through any grief they may be feeling. It begins much like any other meditation—by tuning into your breathing while positioned comfortably. However, because grief is such a powerful emotion, this meditation requires more time to prepare the mind and body. You may also choose to practice this meditation alongside a trusted friend or loved one. This can make you feel safer and more supported during your practice.

When you have focused on your breathing for enough time and feel ready to begin meditating on your grief, bring one hand over your heart. Feel your heartbeat inside of you while you breathe in and out. It is not necessary to breathe as deeply as you can. For this meditation, it is more important that you are comfortable and relaxed. If that means taking soft breaths, you may do so.

With your hand placed on your chest, allow your grief to enter your mind. Take down the barriers you may have put up to prevent your sorrow from overwhelming you. Give yourself permission to cry, feel angry and upset, or simply be in pain. Do not restrict the tears that may come by wiping them away or holding them back. You may weep if that is what your grief needs in order to express itself.

Sit with your grief in this position, holding your heart with love and tenderness. By existing in this moment, you are honoring the sorrow and grief within you and releasing it. Trust that the cycle of your emotions will carry you through this moment and beyond it into a state of openness and acceptance.

There is no need to rush this meditation. Take your time and be patient with the feelings that arise.

Shake Hands With Your Beautiful Monsters

In addition to the dropping technique introduced in Chapter 2, Tsoknyi Rinpoche has also developed an enlightened method for accepting the most intense and difficult emotions. The Tibetan monk encourages his students to view their more extreme reactions to negativity as "beautiful monsters" (Rinpoche, 2023). These beautiful monsters, or overreactions, stem from long-held beliefs that have become distorted over time. Rinpoche provides an example of childhood traumas or misfortunes. If you experienced feelings of worthlessness as a child, you might overreact to unmet expectations or criticisms as an adult. The overreaction that is rooted in a lifetime of self-doubt may manifest as irrational anger or disappointment. This intense overreaction is a beautiful monster.

Tsoknyi Rinpoche places great emphasis on the contradictory nature of the phrase *beautiful monster*. Typically, the word *monster* conjures up images of vicious, terrifying beasts. In childhood, you fear imaginary monsters hiding under your bed. To think of them as beautiful seems bizarre. Your difficult emotions, and subsequent overreactions, are the same. They feel ugly and horrifying, as though they are villains in your mind. However, only referring to them as monsters ignores half of their truth. Rinpoche writes that, by thinking of your negativity as a monster, you are solidifying your aversion and hatred towards it (Rinpoche, 2023). You are not giving it a chance to be more than a painful experience.

To add the word *beautiful* before *monster* shows that you recognize the clarity and spiritual awakening that comes from feeling and accepting difficult emotions. In the same way that your emotions and reactions should not only be considered monsters, they should also not only be considered beautiful. They must be seen for everything that they are, meaning you must recognize their potential to be destructive as well as their potential to be enlightening. They are a difficult but necessary tool for achieving inner peace and genuine joy. Therefore, they are beautiful monsters.

According to Tsoknyi Rinpoche, in order to fully accept your own beautiful monsters, you must become friends with them. The

Buddhist teacher has developed a practice for meeting beautiful monsters with friendliness rather than aversion. He calls it the handshake practice. It is an exercise in sitting with your feelings instead of wishing for them to disappear. True healing happens when you can examine your most difficult emotions without judging them or yourself.

The practice is made up of four steps, plus a dropping practice at the start to prepare your mind. Shaking hands with your beautiful monsters can be a short practice that you attempt every day, every week, or every once in a while. The practice should be exercised with common sense, as well. Many people have experienced significant traumas throughout their life, and the intense feelings that arise in a handshake practice may be overwhelming. Practice this technique in a safe, comforting environment, and do not push your emotional limits to the point where you feel retraumatized.

To begin your handshake practice, refer back to Chapter 2 to perform a simple dropping practice to clear your mind. When finished, take the following steps:

- Step one: Meet all of your emotions, pleasurable and difficult, as if you are inviting them to your home. They are guests in your mind and you are their host. They are not there to cause trouble or hurt you; they are simply there because you invited them. Imagine that these emotions have hands and shake them, welcoming them into your home without judgment. If negativity arises, do not attempt to push it away or kick it out of your home. Acknowledge its presence and move on to welcome the next guest.

- Step two: Practice existing in the same environment as your emotions. Do not try to fix anything that feels uncomfortable, as if you have the cure to an ailment. Nothing needs to be cured. All of your emotions are invited without any hidden agenda. If there is an overwhelming emotion that is difficult to process, such as a beautiful monster, exist with it patiently. If you offer your hand to shake and the beautiful monster meets you with negativity, allow it. Tsoknyi Rinpoche recommends thinking to yourself, *Okay, I am willing to suffer*. Be willing to embrace the beautiful monster for the purpose of overall healing. You do not need to indulge in what the emotion is telling you—it may be ordering you to cease your practice or get angry—because you are choosing to exist with it, not follow its demands. Just allow yourself to be.

- Step three: Practice patience while existing with your emotional guests. This is not a practice that needs to be rushed, nor is it one that has an end goal that you must accomplish. You are simply holding space for your emotions. Meditate in this mindset for a length of time that feels right to you. Take this time to relax with your pleasurable emotions and beautiful monsters.

- Step four: After you have held enough space in your mind to feel comfortable existing with all of your emotions, you can begin to communicate with them. Allow any questions to be asked and answered through an objective lens. Remind your emotions, particularly the more difficult ones to process, that they are valid. They exist for a reason and they are real, but that does not mean they are true. If there is fear or worry inside of you, remind it that its narrative is one of emotion, not undeniable fact. Tell your emotions that they have been received with open arms and acceptance. Tell yourself that there is nothing inside of you that needs to be fixed or cured. From here, you can open yourself up to the wisdom that exists within every emotion.

Practice these steps as often as you would like, and as you establish healthy relationships with your intense feelings and thoughts, you will begin to feel the transformation. The purpose of this practice is to heal through acceptance and self-compassion.

Chapter 6:

Choosing to Rest

Give Yourself a Break

No matter how kind you are or how often you practice generosity and altruism, you can only reach your own enlightenment when you also allow yourself to rest. Although the Buddhist philosophy places a heavy emphasis on putting others' well-being over one's own, it does not imply that you should stop caring for yourself completely. In order to practice ancient techniques and treat others well, you have to be able to support yourself. The difference between supporting yourself and being self-involved is how you view your identity. If you see your well-being as more important than others, you are self-involved. Yet, if you see your well-being as equally important and necessary to maintain as you see the well-being of others, you are supporting yourself while maintaining Buddhist values.

Being compassionate toward yourself means giving yourself what you need to survive. Food, water, and shelter are undeniable for your survival, but so is sufficient rest. You cannot grow or heal from suffering if you do not take the time to rest peacefully.

Meditation, as you have learned, is a great tool for opening the mind and developing inner peace. Therefore, it is also a great tool for resting your mind and body. When you feel at peace, your rushing thoughts and jittery energy are on pause. You may not be asleep, but you are resting.

Think about a time when you were so overwhelmed and stressed out that all you wanted to do was lay on your bed and take a nap. That is your body and mind's way of telling you it is time to rest. It is not that you are lazy or unmotivated, something many people fear due to our society's infatuation with hustling. Your body and mind deserve a moment of rest so that they can come back into their naturally peaceful states. The jitteriness you feel so often is a reaction to the stressors in your life. By actively choosing to rest before your body forces you to, you are giving yourself power over your well-being instead of giving power to the things that stress you out.

Resting also resets your energy to a more palatable state rather than one that drives you crazy. Your brain functions better after rest through both conscious and unconscious forms. It is a known fact that a good night's sleep allows a person to perform better throughout the day—in more ways than one. Healthy sleep schedules help people focus on their work, nourish their short and long-term memories, and boost their moods. Meditation provides similar benefits. In one scientific study of the effects of meditation, researchers found that mindfulness practices can improve a person's concentration, alertness, and wakefulness (Britton et al., 2013). The study showed that meditation is a practice that wakes people up, causing the research contributors to affectionately title their study *Awakening Is Not A Metaphor*, referring to the Buddhist use of the term "awakening."

It is important to note that resting the mind and resting the body are two different practices. While it is easy to assume that laying down for a quick nap is a good way to rest the mind *and* body, it can sometimes make our minds even more restless than before. How many times have you tried to go to sleep, feeling the familiar exhaustion deep in your bones, but have been kept awake by the thoughts racing through your mind? When that happens, how difficult is it to get those thoughts to settle?

It's possible that a person's conscious efforts to silence the mind in these moments will actually make the restlessness worse. You begin to grow frustrated at your mind's persistence, tossing and turning in your bed with the hope that you will find a position comfortable enough to induce sleep faster and quiet your mind. All of this back and forth going on inside you, in the meantime, is only making you more unable to fall asleep. Soon, so much time has passed that you eventually fall asleep much later than you intended, damaging your sleep schedule—and your mood for the next day.

Being aware of the many ways of combating excessive mental energy is the first step to getting rest.

Procrastination and Distraction

Have you ever heard the phrase "revenge bedtime procrastination"? It is derived from a Chinese expression used to communicate one's frustration about long, stressful workdays (Suni, 2021). Now that it has gained popularity among native-English speakers, the phrase has connected with a bigger community. The English use of the phrase signifies a person's refusal to go to sleep after a day of work so that they have more time to do the activities they enjoy since they are unable to do them earlier. The "revenge" part comes from the notion that a person is sacrificing a sufficient night's sleep to avenge the time they sacrificed to work or deal with stressful responsibilities. Basically, revenge bedtime procrastination is a way for someone to stay up late doing what they want, despite losing sleep because of it.

According to Eric Suni of the Sleep Foundation (2023), genuine revenge bedtime procrastination involves three things: the awareness that negative consequences will follow a night of insufficient sleep; a lack of valid reason to stay up later than required; and, of course, a delay in one's total amount of time spent sleeping. Reasons that would not be considered valid for staying up late are scrolling on social media, watching television, or other non-essential activities.

Revenge bedtime procrastination can result in serious consequences, most of which could be avoided with a good night's sleep. As you have already learned, poor sleep can lead to memory problems, unstable moods, and difficulty concentrating. Those who participate in this type of procrastination are likely making their daily life more difficult for themselves. Though the concept is too new to researchers to involve various statistics, Suni references a study that revealed that women and students most commonly engage in bedtime procrastination.

Another challenge many people face in their lives is the constant need to be distracted from their thoughts. This problem can arise for a multitude of reasons, ranging from overwhelming feelings to severe mental health concerns. In fact, mental illnesses like depression and anxiety can cause people so much emotional anguish that they develop a dependency on quick distractions. Through distractions, people suffering from mental illnesses can get a quick boost of dopamine and focus their troubled minds on less intense content. There are even people who use their phones to dissociate from themselves, meaning they are able to disconnect from the ways their bodies and minds feel (Maniaci, 2021). Today, mindless scrolling on smartphones, binge-watching television shows, and overusing drugs and alcohol are some of the many distractions people depend on.

The Covid-19 pandemic also had a major impact on society's desire for technological distraction. In what has been labeled a "digital surge," people have become more connected to their devices and technologies than at any other time in history (De' et al., 2020). People affected by the pandemic initially turned to technology for various reasons, including for the ability to communicate while remaining socially distant and to stay entertained while being quarantined at home. Soon after the pandemic took hold of societal norms, utilizing technology to complete daily tasks became commonplace. Groceries were able to be ordered online and delivered without in-person contact, many employees were given the option to work from home, and students attended school online.

It is more than likely that you have your own experiences with this unprecedented phenomenon. The digital surge has provided opportunities that were unheard of merely decades ago, many of which have benefited humanity. Yet, there are many disadvantages brought on by the increased dependence on digital technology. For starters, the rates of online scams have increased and people with limited access to the internet have faced extreme social exclusion. In addition, people are becoming more and more reliant on their phones, tablets, computers, and the internet in general. Such a heavy dependency on these devices, though common today, has the ability to completely alter the human brain's ability to concentrate.

In a study conducted to better understand human distractedness, researchers found that, on average, a person's attention to a screen only lasted about 74 seconds. After that time passed, people's focus switched to something else. This was in 2012. Between 2016 and 2021, this amount of time decreased to a shocking 47 seconds (Hunt, 2023). Less than one minute and the average human brain needs something new to put its attention on. The researchers who discovered this information say such short attention spans are a direct cause of new technology. A vicious cycle has begun, one in which our attention is influenced by the use of new tech, and new tech is influenced by our decreasing ability to pay attention. With this in mind, it makes sense that short-form videos and quick-to-read content have become so popular in recent years.

Now that distractions are so easy to find, people who feel unhappy and unfulfilled are becoming addicted. Constantly searching for distractions to replace emotional problems teaches one's brain to crave dopamine, a feel-good chemical in the human brain. Dopamine is released in several different ways, such as by eating a tasty snack or watching funny videos on social networking sites. By using these activities to distract yourself from your problems, you are essentially turning your brain into a casino. However, instead of winning money, you win dopamine boosts.

With every video you scroll to on your phone, you're taking an emotional gamble. Will the next video be good enough to make you laugh, distracting you from the negative or overwhelming thoughts in your mind? Hoping that it will, you scroll to find out. If the video is successful in boosting your dopamine, you take a chance on the next video, and the next, and the next. After a while, you've watched so many quick videos that you have been thoroughly distracted, but your negative thoughts are just waiting on the sidelines for their moment to come back.

Of course, this is a very specific example. Some people have strict boundaries with social media and internet use, yet they have other distractions that serve the same purpose. It does not matter what is used to cause the distraction, though. As long as you are ignoring your true problems and seeking temporary happiness through distractions, you will never truly feel joyful.

Not only does distraction from negative thoughts go against Buddhist philosophy, but it also does more harm than good. While a momentary distraction can feel good, it works the same way as instant gratification. It brings a brief feeling of happiness, only to allow reality to come crashing in when the distraction is taken away. Instead of trying to replace your worries with distractions, try replacing them with meaningful activities. This is where Buddhist practices can be of great help.

For many, the act of renouncing distractions can manifest as simple meditation. When one meditates, one is training their mind to free itself from its own distractibility. Jetsun Khandro Rinpoche, a renowned bhikkhuni, often teaches her students about the power that comes from renouncing distractions, particularly through meditation. Her approach toward the practice is unique in that she emphasizes one's yearning while they meditate. In 2010, while speaking to her students, Jetsun Khandro Rinpoche said that meditation requires "a yearning for the mind to become strong enough not to be constantly distracted or diverted into creating causes of samsara," or a cycle of suffering (Jetsun Khandro Rinpoche, 2010).

Exercises for Rest

Yoga Nidra

Yoga nidra is a powerful relaxation tool that can help you restore your energy and help you feel ready to take on the day. Despite its name, the practice is not your typical yoga session. You do not need to be an experienced yogi to perform yoga nidra correctly, nor do you have to have impressive flexibility or balancing skills.

The meaning of *yoga nidra*, which has been used in Hindu and Buddhist practices for centuries, is twofold. The term *yoga* is derived from a Sanskrit word meaning unity and connection. When discussing yoga nidra, specifically, the term is used to signify the yogic position one is in when practicing. The term *nidra* comes from the Sanskrit word for sleep. When used together, *yoga nidra* becomes the name of the ancient practice of restoring one's energy in a state between being awake and asleep (The Yoga Nomads, 2022).

The practice of yoga nidra is similar to meditation in that it requires a person to be consciously aware and set intentions; however, it is different from typical meditative practices in many ways. Female spiritual teacher and master of enlightenment, Anandmurti Gurumaa, describes the practice as an "ancient tantric method which can open latent potentiality of the mind" (Gurumaa, 2020). First and foremost, yoga nidra is always performed in a laying-down position, called the corpse pose or *savasana*. If you have ever taken a yoga class before, you may be familiar with savasana as the final position of the practice. When practicing savasana, a person will lie on their back with their eyes closed and arms extended comfortably along the sides of their body. It is a position known for its relaxing and calming effects.

Yoga nidra is also a guided practice, meaning an instructor should be present to verbally guide you through the exercise. Many people prefer in-person instructions, though you can find several videos of guided yoga nidra practices online. The practice follows a series of individual steps that take you through the process of connecting with your conscious mind, body, and inner self. A typical guided yoga nidra session should last somewhere between 30 and 45 minutes. With regular meditation and simple stretching, a practice can be as short as you like. However, with yoga nidra, it should not be any shorter than 20 minutes, as you need plenty of time to delve into your consciousness.

In a full 45-minute yoga nidra session, you can expect to follow eight steps, as defined by Swami Satyananda Saraswati, a modern spiritual teacher (The Yoga Nomads, 2022). Simply put, the eight steps are:

1. Internalization: Finding a relaxing, comfortable position and focusing on your breathing while releasing initial tension in your body.

2. Sankalpa: *Sankalpa*, meaning *intention*, is when you identify your individual purpose for your yoga nidra session.

3. Body Scan: Practicing mindfulness throughout your body by focusing your attention on each body part and briefly feeling any sensations it has.

4. Breath Awareness: Focusing on your breathing and practicing slow, steady inhales and exhales.

5. Opposites: Mentally acknowledging contradicting sensations within yourself, such as feelings of heaviness and lightness.

6. Visualization: Imagining various images and scenarios in your mind to encourage your creative abilities and disconnect from negative thought processes.

7. Sankalpa: Revisiting your initial intentions and repeatedly reciting them to yourself.

8. Externalization: Bringing yourself out of your high level of consciousness and returning to your physical body and experiences by focusing on your breathing and senses.

By following these steps with the guidance of your instructor, you will enter a state of consciousness and awareness that you might not usually access. Yoga nidra is a wonderful method for feeling well-rested, particularly after a poor night's sleep or a tiring day. Keep in mind, though, that it should not be practiced as a way to replace your sleep every night completely. Think of it more as a mental coffee break—one that fills you with awareness and genuine energy instead of jitteriness and caffeine.

Methods for Better Sleep

Thai Buddhist monk, Nick Keomahavong, has a YouTube channel dedicated to sharing Buddhist wisdom and practices with the world. In one video titled *How to Get Better Sleep*, Keomahavong discusses his recommended methods for achieving restful, energizing sleep. So many people in the world suffer from poor sleep schedules and practices, making them more exhausted and frustrated throughout their days. If you identify with this issue, the following methods may be beneficial for you to experiment with.

Keomahavong's first piece of advice is to treat your sleeping area as it was originally meant to be treated: as a place to sleep. A common habit among people today is using their bedroom as a workspace or catch-all room, filling the area with items that ultimately distract a person from sleeping. By choosing to work on your laptop and paperwork in bed or by having piles of unwashed clothes on the floor, what was once a peaceful room will become a reminder of overwhelming and burdensome tasks. In many cases, just having a television in the bedroom discourages healthy sleep.

To combat this, try reframing your bedroom's purpose. Complete your work in other rooms, maintain a clean space around your bed, and "teach your mind that getting in bed means going to sleep" (Hostakova, 2022).

Nick Keomahavong also advises people to maintain a consistent sleep time. Not only does this mean falling asleep at the same time every night, but it also means avoiding any daytime naps. Though it may be tempting to rest your eyes in the middle of the day or stay up later than usual watching your favorite show, inconsistencies in your sleep schedule will make it harder for you to sleep regularly. If you practice falling asleep or trying to fall asleep at the same time each night, it will eventually become a habit that your body and mind will enjoy. In his video, Keomahavong explains that the monks in his monastery have a strict bedtime every night. This is not because they are being forced to sleep or because there will be any sort of punishment. Rather, they do this to achieve consistent energy levels and maximize their mental awareness during the day.

In addition, Keomahavong and his fellow monks ensure that they make their beds every morning as soon as they have woken up and begun their day. The purpose of this practice is to create a neat, pleasing environment, as well as develop the habit of "finishing the job" of sleeping. Having a neatly made bed helps move the events of the day forward and prevents you from returning to sleep before your set bedtime. He also states that the act of making the bed symbolizes the idea that you have the ability to see a problem, find a solution, and continue on with your day (Keomahavong, 2020).

A more surprising piece of advice from the Thai monk is to not make your bed or sleeping space *too* comfortable. It may feel nice to have an exceptionally soft blanket, luxurious mattress, and fluffy pillows when you sleep, but these items make it even more difficult to get up in the morning. You have surely experienced a morning in which you truly did not want to get out of your bed, whether it was because you were so comfortable or because you knew you would feel cold and grumpy when you removed your blankets. No matter what it is that holds you back from wanting to rise from bed, it is inhibiting you from feeling motivated and grateful for a new day to live.

Finally, and most importantly, Nick Keomahavong emphasizes the role of the last thought you have before falling asleep. His own teacher taught him that your last waking thought of the day or night becomes your first waking thought the next morning. Therefore, if you fall asleep to the thought of all your mistakes or disappointments of the day, you will wake up still thinking about them. In the same way, if you go to bed feeling overwhelmed with negativity or thoughts of *I should have...*, you will be consumed by the same ideas the following morning.

Instead of ending your day or night on a negative note, try falling asleep to thoughts of gratitude and positive reflection. Keomahavong also recommends reflecting on the good deeds and moments of pride you felt during the day so that you wake up feeling fulfilled and ready to have another positive experience. The monk considers this practice a way of sleeping in a "sea of merit" (Keomahavong, 2020).

Following one or more of these Buddhist monk-approved practices may be the antidote to exhaustion that you have been yearning for.

Stepping Away From Your Devices

The simple practice of taking time away from your devices can have a significant impact on your well-being. If you are someone who finds themselves mindlessly scrolling through their phone or tablet while doing other activities, such as eating meals or completing household chores, you will greatly benefit from this exercise.

The first thing you need to be aware of is *why* you crave additional distractions when performing tasks. Is it for the small dopamine boosts you receive when watching videos while cooking dinner or folding laundry? Do you need background noise while working from home, otherwise you get too caught up in your own thoughts? Are you used to being overstimulated by endless responsibilities or kids running around the house to the point that doing one task in silence is unnerving?

There are countless reasons for your desire to keep your mind overly occupied. The point of the matter is that you identify the true cause or causes. Once you become aware of why you want to be distracted or overstimulated, you can learn to become more mindful and regain your ability to focus on one thing at a time. Doing multiple things at once can feel more productive, but it comes at the cost of not giving each task your full, genuine attention. When you do practice singular focus, you are aligning yourself with the Buddhist practice of mindfulness.

So, what does all of this mean? In short, it means that you may need to exercise freedom from what provides you with limitless distractions. This may be your smartphone, tablet, laptop, or television; whatever it is that keeps you from focusing on one thing at a time.

Some effective ways of separating yourself from your devices are to implement set times throughout your day when you will step away. This could be a handful of 15-minute breaks during which you practice a walking meditation or an hour at the end of your day when you can complete tasks without technology. If you frequently stay up late using your phone while lying in bed, you could make a rule for yourself not to use your phone before bed. Instead, you could spend the last portion of your evening reading a good book, talking with your partner or children, or journaling about the events of your day. That way, when it is time for you to close your eyes, you can feel a sense of accomplishment for doing technology and distraction-free activity. This will also free your mind from focusing on the chaos of daily life, which you can often be reminded of when looking at social media, news sources, or even the calendar app on your phone.

For the women who struggle to put their devices aside because of the temptation to browse social media apps or play digital games, you can set a timer to signify when to do a digital detox. Some smartphones even allow you to set time limits on your apps, alerting you when you have reached your limit and turning off the application. It may be beneficial for you to set tangible limits for yourself in this way.

If all else fails, try physically abandoning your devices, even for a short time. Leave your phone in one room and go to another to practice the many Buddhist exercises in this book. You may even want to leave your phone inside your house and go outside or take a drive in your car. However you can realistically spend time away from your digital distractions and rest—whether you are resting your mind, body, or both—will give you a chance to clear your mind and focus on inner peace and relaxation.

Conclusion

Take a deep breath. Notice how your lungs accept the intake of air eagerly. In a similar way, your mind has just accepted the wisdom of the Buddha with true dedication. Now that you have reached the end of this particular journey, you can rejoice in the fact that you have undergone an intense spiritual transformation. Whether you are aware of it now or not, the lessons you have learned throughout this book will stick with you in one way or another.

As a woman in the 21st century, you will undoubtedly face difficult times in your daily life. The pressure from others to behave in a certain way, the demands of your career, and the mental load that comes from raising a family can weigh you down. All of the responsibilities you are saddled with, along with the maintenance of your own health and well-being, have the potential to outshine your happiness. On top of that, many of these responsibilities cannot, and should not, be ignored. What you *can* do, however, is train your mind to embrace and accept all that happens to you, whether it is positive or negative.

When you become overwhelmed with sadness, you may think back to the Buddha's words on suffering and how it cannot be avoided, but it can be turned into a lesson. In moments of pure happiness and satisfaction, you may remember to express your gratitude for a pleasurable experience. Most importantly, when you feel as though you are stuck in an emotional prison, you may remember that there are ways to free yourself and unburden your mind.

At the beginning of this book, you were introduced to Siddhartha Gautama, a young prince who had never known the meaning of suffering. You learned about his journey of enlightenment, during which he abandoned the luxuries he was accustomed to and lived a life of poverty. You gained a better understanding of his evolving belief system that eventually established him as the Buddha. From the inevitability of suffering to the effects of karma, you became aware of what it means to live a life inspired by Buddhism.

From there, you were taught about happiness and genuine joy. The Westernized beliefs you may have held were challenged by the Buddhist idea that happiness can only come from within instead of from material possessions or social luxuries. You learned that, regardless of the amount of suffering in the world, genuine joy is always within reach. Through breathing techniques developed by experienced Buddhist monks, meditations that encourage detachment, and the art of mindfulness, you can achieve levels of happiness you never knew were possible.

In Chapter 3, free will and mental freedom were discussed. Though scholars, scientists, and Buddhists have varying views on the idea of free will, you learned the one truth that remains: meditation is liberation. By taking the time to practice meditation and mindfulness, you can liberate your mind from negative thoughts and worries. You were provided with methods for achieving your own mental freedom, as well as given wisdom from world-renowned Buddhist teachers. You learned that living with authenticity and acceptance is the key to living freely.

Chapter 4 delved into the art of compassionate action, or Karuna, something that every Buddhist must develop. Any beliefs about the egoic "self" were dismantled by the truth that all human beings are interconnected. You were taught about the Buddha's hope for all humans to treat each other as equals and stand in solidarity in order to establish collective peace. The importance of compassion was emphasized by the wisdom that developing Karuna is a way of alleviating human suffering. You learned that true compassion is made up of solidarity, forgiveness, and gratitude. Most importantly, true compassion means showing yourself the same respect and kindness that you show others. It may be difficult, but self-compassion is just as important as any other aspect of Buddhist philosophy.

Following the discussion of compassion, Chapter 5 taught you how to manage your most difficult emotions. For so many people, negativity has begun to outweigh positivity, leaving them feeling hopeless and depressed. While some emotions are natural, such as disappointment and anger, excess negativity acts like poison to one's mind and body. You learned that your excess emotions and overreactions are beautiful monsters living in your mind. They may seem scary and ugly at first glance, but they serve a meaningful purpose for your well-being. In Chapter 5, you were introduced to Tsoknyi Rinpoche's handshake practice, where you become friends with your own beautiful monsters instead of enemies. You were also introduced to various breathing exercises, meditations, and the Dalai Lama's Atlas of Emotions, all tools that you can greatly benefit from every day.

Finally, you reached Chapter 6, the final section of this book. In this chapter, after the influx of information and wisdom you were given previously, you were taught to rest. The type of rest encouraged by Buddhist teachers is not the same as taking a nap when you are tired or ignoring your responsibilities until you are overwhelmed. Rather, Buddhists perceive rest as a way to give your mind and body a well-deserved break. This type of rest can mean distancing yourself from social media and mobile devices, meditating before bed, practicing yoga nidra, or redesigning your sleeping environment. With these techniques, you will be able to regain your energy and feel more ready than ever to get through your busy schedule.

Whether you connect with all of the techniques in this book or a select few, you are deeply encouraged to use the knowledge you have learned as often as possible. The tools you have been given are meant to be implemented as needed throughout your daily life. Gaining knowledge is a great start, but your spiritual transformation will truly start when you practice what you have learned and develop your skills. You do not need to have the desire to become a Buddha; you only need to know that you have the power to create a happier life for yourself.

Glossary

Asceticism: A way of life that prevents one from indulging in materialistic or personal pleasures through extreme self-denial and discipline.

Bhikkhuni: A female member of the Buddhist community, also referred to as a Buddhist nun.

Dakini: A Sanskrit word meaning "sky dancer" or "sky dweller"; in Buddhist teachings, a Dakini represents a wise female with liberating energy.

Determinism: The theory that every person's fate, including that of humanity as a whole, is uncontrollable and predetermined by a larger force.

Dharma: The essential concept of Buddhist teachings.

Duhkha: Frequently mentioned in Buddhist scripture, a word meaning a combination of suffering, unhappiness, and pain.

Enlightenment: The state that occurs when one achieves the goals of Buddhism, gaining insight into the Four Noble Truths and reaching the end of the karmic life cycle.

Free Will: A person's ability to act as they choose, without being restricted by an uncontrollable fate or destiny.

Interdependence: The metaphysical connection between all human beings, regardless of physical location.

Karma: The idea that one's mental, emotional, and physical actions come with consequences, both good and bad; a person's destiny is decided by their choices in life and past lives.

Karuna: The Buddhist concept of compassion and sympathy toward oneself and others.

Magga: The Sanskrit word that represents the method of ending suffering by following the Eightfold Path.

Mantra: A meaningful word or phrase that encourages focus on one's emotional intentions, typically during meditative practices.

Meditation: An exercise in which one relaxes the body and focuses on breathing and remaining mindful, often accompanied by a mantra or chant.

Maitri: The Sanskrit word that refers to the concept of loving-kindness, goodwill, and benevolence, similar to the Pali word metta.

Mindfulness: The practice of being aware of the present moment and focusing on what currently is, rather than what was or what could be.

Monastery: A religious community and residence for monks and nuns to live away from society to practice their religion.

Monk: A male member of a religious community, typically residing in a monastery, who dedicates his life to his religious beliefs and practices; someone who has given up worldly materials and lifestyles to devote his life to his religion.

Nirodha: The Sanskrit word representing the idea that suffering can be overcome.

Nirvana: The ultimate goal of Buddhism, in which one reaches complete enlightenment and happiness—a final release from suffering, karma, and the cycle of life and rebirth.

Nun: A female member of a religious community, typically residing in a monastery, who dedicates her life to her religious beliefs and practices; someone who has given up worldly materials and lifestyles to devote her life to her religion.

Prajna: The Sanskrit word that refers to one's level of wisdom and enlightenment.

Samadhi: The Sanskrit word that refers to one's process of mental evolution, concentration, and meditation.

Samsara: The Sanskrit word that represents the idea that humans exist in a cycle of life, death, and rebirth until they reach enlightenment.

Samudaya: The Sanskrit word that represents the cause of suffering.

Savasana: A pose in yoga, often referred to as the "corpse pose," in which the practitioner closes their eyes while lying on their back with their arms comfortably extended along their sides.

Shamatha: The Sanskrit word that refers to the simplest form of meditation, meaning tranquility and peaceful abiding.

Sila: The Sanskrit word used in Buddhist philosophy that refers to one's morality, good virtues, and reciprocity to others.

Zen: A state of mind and philosophy that focuses on inner peace and intuition, typically found through meditation and other Buddhist practices.

Thank You

Dear Reader, thank you for taking the time to read my book.

If you enjoyed this book and have a moment to spare. I'd be forever grateful for a review.

Your thoughts help Authors like me grow, continue writing and help prospective readers too.

About the Author

Born a Buddhist, Priya Roshan has spent over 30 years learning and practicing the teachings of the Buddha. She has witnessed firsthand the incredible impact Buddhism has on people's lives, millennia after this religious movement began. Being a mom, Priya balances work and family life every day. She understands that life can be busy and sometimes chaotic. She hopes to show women how to adapt the life-changing teachings of Buddhism to their own lives. From busy moms to stressed-out students, Priya's personal experiences and lessons learned will show you that balance is possible.

References

Bassis, K. (2020, February 27). *Feelings and emotions.* Berkeley Buddhist Priory. https://berkeleybuddhistpriory.org/2020/02/27/feelings-and-emotions/

Bhattacharya, R. (2017, November 2). *Understanding Buddhism through a feminist lens.* Feminism in India. https://feminisminindia.com/2017/11/03/understanding-buddhism-feminist-lens/

Britton, W. B., Lindahl, J. R., Cahn, B. R., Davis, J. H., & Goldman, R. E. (2013). Awakening is not a metaphor: the effects of Buddhist meditation practices on basic wakefulness. *Annals of the New York Academy of Sciences, 1307*(1), 64–81. https://doi.org/10.1111/nyas.12279

Buddhism for beginners. (2023). Dharma Wisdom. https://dharmawisdom.org/buddhism-for-beginners/

Buddhism. (2022). *How to do karuna meditation: Buddhism in English* [Video]. YouTube. https://www.youtube.com/watch?v=WnUhg0DI9mY

Buddhist concept of happiness. (2022). Bhāvanā Society. https://bhavanasociety.org/buddhist-concept-of-happiness/

Champion, L. (2019, December 11). *How to practice gratitude, according to 3 Buddhist monks.* PureWow. https://www.purewow.com/wellness/how-to-practice-gratitude

Chu, M. (2017, July 10). *Why your brain prioritizes instant gratification over long-term goals, according to science.* Inc. Australia. https://www.inc-aus.com/melissa-chu/why-your-brain-prioritizes-instant-gratification-o.html

Compassion. (n.d.). The Center for Compassion and Altruism Research and Education; Stanford Medicine. http://ccare.stanford.edu/research/wiki/compassion-definitions/compassion/#:~:text=Compassion%20%E2%80%9CIn%20the%20classical%20teachings

De', R., Pandey, N., & Pal, A. (2020). Impact of digital surge during Covid-19 pandemic: A viewpoint on research and practice. *International Journal of Information Management, 55*(102171), 102171. NCBI. https://doi.org/10.1016/j.ijinfomgt.2020.102171

Depression: Distraction, activities and creativity. (2017). Health Talk. https://healthtalk.org/depression/depression-distraction-activities-and-creativity

Essentials of Buddhism: Key concepts of Buddhism. (2022). Buddha Web. http://buddhaweb.org/

Federman, A. (2010). What kind of free will did the Buddha teach? *Philosophy East and West, 60*(1), 1-19. https://www.jstor.org/stable/40469162?searchText=&searchUri=&ab_segments=&searchKey=&refreqid=fastly-default%3Ab0b5f4de7b875f4fc48099d00be6da25

Fronsdal, G. (2023). *The practice of generosity.* Insight Meditation Center. https://www.insightmeditationcenter.org/the-practice-of-generosity/#:~:text=At%20its%20most%20basic%20level

Fundamental teachings. (2023). The Buddhist Society. https://www.thebuddhistsociety.org/page/fundamental-teachings

Godoy, M., & Nguyen, A. (2022, June 16). *Stop doomscrolling and get ready for bed: Here's how to reclaim a good night's sleep.* NPR. https://www.npr.org/2022/06/14/1105122521/stop-revenge-bedtime-procrastination-get-better-sleep

Gregoire, C. (2014, May 19). *Jack Kornfield on gratitude and mindfulness.* Greater Good Magazine. https://greatergood.berkeley.edu/article/item/jack_kornfield_on_gratitude_and_mindfulness

Gurumaa, A. (2020). *Yoga nidra: Guided meditation to relax, rejuvenate and reform.* [Video]. YouTube. https://www.youtube.com/watch?v=n_ce66a9MV0

Health Assured Team. (2023, February 27). *Women's mental health: The statistics.* Health Assured. https://www.healthassured.org/blog/women-s-mental-health-the-statistics/

History.com Editors. (2020a, April 7). *Buddhists celebrate birth of Gautama Buddha.* History; A&E Television Networks. https://www.history.com/this-day-in-history/buddhists-celebrate-birth-of-gautama-buddha

History.com Editors. (2020b, July 22). *Buddhism.* History; A&E Television Networks. https://www.history.com/topics/religion/buddhism

Hostakova, S. (2022, January 17). *4 simple Buddhist methods for better sleep and restful mornings.* Medium; Better Advice. https://medium.com/better-advice/4-simple-buddhist-methods-for-better-sleep-and-restful-mornings-95eaa5a9519e

Hunt, E. (2023, January 1). *Is modern life ruining our powers of concentration?* The Guardian. https://www.theguardian.com/technology/2023/jan/01/is-modern-life-ruining-our-powers-of-concentration

Jank, W. (2022, November 7). *The 7 oldest religions in the world.* World Atlas. https://www.worldatlas.com/religion/the-7-oldest-religions-in-the-world.html

Jetsun Khandro Rinpoche. (2010). *This precious opportunity*. Khandro Rinpoche. https://www.khandrorinpoche.org/teachings/print/jkr-this-precious-opportunity-2010-12-31/

Keomahavong, N. (2020). *How to get better sleep* [Video]. YouTube. https://www.youtube.com/watch?v=b47Wz6odqek

Kham, P. (2023). *Stopping, calming, resting, healing*. Applied Buddhism. https://appliedbuddhism.org/th/mindfulness-practices/foundation-of-mindfulness/234-stopping-calming-resting-healing

King, E. (2022, May 26). *Cultivating Karuna*. Still Water Mindfulness Practice Center. https://www.stillwatermpc.org/dharma-topics/cultivating-karuna/

Kornfield, J. (2017, September 13). *A meditation on grief*. Jack Kornfield. https://jackkornfield.com/meditation-grief/

Kornfield, J. (2022, July 12). *Gratitude and wonder*. Jack Kornfield. https://jackkornfield.com/gratitude/#:~:text=Gratitude%20is%20a%20gracious%20acknowledgment

Labde, A. (2021, April 21). *Women's participation in Buddhism*. Feminism in India. https://feminisminindia.com/2021/04/22/women-participation-in-buddhism/#:~:text=The%20Buddha%20emphasises%20the

Lama, D., Tutu, D., & Abrams, D. (2016). *The book of joy: Lasting happiness in a changing world.* Avery, An Imprint Of Penguin Random House.

Maniaci, M. (2021, November 6). *Endless distraction: Smartphones as a coping mechanism.* Medium; Thing A Day. https://medium.com/thing-a-day/endless-distraction-smartphones-as-a-coping-mechanism-f021421e3ef

Mark, J. (2020, September 25). *Buddhism.* World History Encyclopedia. https://www.worldhistory.org/buddhism/

Mead, E. (2019, May 27). *The history and origin of meditation.* Positive Psychology. https://positivepsychology.com/history-of-meditation/#:~:text=The%20Buddha%20(India)&text=Buddhism%20texts%20refer%20to%20many

Merriam-Webster. (2023). Freedom. In *Merriam-Webster.com dictionary.* Retrieved April 25, 2023. https://www.merriam-webster.com/dictionary/freedom?utm_campaign=sd&utm_medium=serp&utm_source=jsonld

Moffitt, P. (2021, February 9). *Dharma wisdom with Phillip Moffitt: Disappointment.* Soundcloud. https://dharmawisdom.org/disappointment/

Morrison, E. (2020, October 25). *The meaning and benefits behind the popular Om Mani Padme Hum yoga mantra.* Yoga Practice. https://yogapractice.com/yoga/om-mani-padme-hum/#:~:text=Om%20Mani%20Padme%20Hum%20is

Nakamura, H., Kitagawa, J. M., Llewelyn Snellgrove, D., Reynolds, F. E., Lopez, D. S., & Tucci, G. (2023). *Buddhism: Foundations, history, systems, mythology, and practice*. In Encyclopædia Britannica. https://www.britannica.com/topic/Buddhism

National Geographic. (2023). *Buddhism.* Education | National Geographic. https://education.nationalgeographic.org/resource/buddhism/

O'Brien, B. (2018a, July 8). *Learn the importance of compassion or karuna in Buddhism.* Learn Religions. https://www.learnreligions.com/buddhism-and-compassion-449719

O'Brien, B. (2018b, August 26). *An examination of free will and Buddhism.* Learn Religions. https://www.learnreligions.com/free-will-and-buddhism-449602

O'Brien, B. (2020, January 2). *The practice of loving kindness.* Learn Religions. https://www.learnreligions.com/loving-kindness-metta-449703

Ohnuma, R. (2023). *Professor Ohnuma on Buddhism and nature of mothering.* Department of Religion; Trustees of Dartmouth College. https://religion.dartmouth.edu/news/2013/05/professor-ohnuma-buddhism-and-nature-mothering

Parachin, V. M. (2023). *6 tools for more freedom: The Buddhist way.* Spirituality & Health. https://www.spiritualityhealth.com/articles/2021/03/17/6-tools-for-more-freedom-the-buddhist-way

Phramaha Nopadol Saisuta, V. (2012). *The Buddhist core values and perspectives for protection challenges: Faith and protection.* UNHCR. https://www.unhcr.org/media/buddhist-core-values-and-perspectives-protection-challenges-faith-and-protection

Piver, S. (2008). *Quiet mind: a beginner's guide to meditation.* Shambhala.

Piver, S., Maezen Miller, K., & Fischer, N. (2022, October 20). *How 3 Buddhist teachers work with difficult emotions.* Lion's Roar. https://www.lionsroar.com/how-3-buddhist-teachers-work-with-difficult-emotions/

Plum Village. (2023, January 17). *Freedom in every smile: Parallel verses for the Lunar New Year.* Plum Village. https://plumvillage.org/articles/freedom-in-every-smile-parallel-verses-for-the-lunar-new-year/

Rasicot, C. (2021). *To walk proudly as Buddhist women: An interview with Dhammananda Bhikkhuni.* Lion's Roar. https://www.lionsroar.com/to-walk-proudly-as-buddhist-women-an-interview-with-dhammananda-bhikkhuni/

Razzetti, G. (2019, February 15). *Dalai Lama has the antidote to destructive emotions.* Fearless Culture. https://www.fearlessculture.design/blog-posts/dalai-lama-has-the-antidote-to-destructive-emotions

Reiki Administrator. (2015, March 25). *The meaning of Karuna.* Reiki; The International Center for Reiki Training. https://www.reiki.org/meaning-karuna

Repetti, R. (2010). *Meditation and mental freedom: A Buddhist theory of free will.* In CUNY Academic Works. https://academicworks.cuny.edu/cgi/viewcontent.cgi?article=1119&context=kb_pubs

Repetti, R. (2012). *Buddhist hard determinism: No self, no free will, no responsibility.* In CUNY Academic Works. https://academicworks.cuny.edu/cgi/viewcontent.cgi?article=1115&context=kb_pubs

Ribeiro, M. (2019, July 4). *What is compassion meditation?* Positive Psychology. https://positivepsychology.com/compassion-meditation/

Ricard, M. (2014). A Buddhist view of happiness. *Journal of Law and Religion, 29*(1), 14–29. https://doi.org/10.1017/jlr.2013.9

Rider, K. J. (2020, July 14). *What the Buddha taught us about disappointment.* Medium. https://kerryjrider.medium.com/what-the-buddha-taught-us-about-disappointment-b68dcde03151#:~:text=Buddha%20tells%20us%20that%20our

Rinpoche, A. (2021, April 12). *The 4 noble truths of emotional suffering.* Lion's Roar. https://www.lionsroar.com/the-4-noble-truths-of-emotional-suffering/#:~:text=In%20the%20Buddhist%20teachings%2C%20we

Rinpoche, T. (2022, December 10). How to be happy with Tsoknyi Rinpoche and Daniel Goleman (The Investor's Podcast Network & D. Goleman, Interviewers) [Interview]. In *The Investor's Podcast Network.* https://www.theinvestorspodcast.com/richer-wiser-happier/how-to-be-happy-w-tsoknyi-rinpoche-daniel-goleman/

Rinpoche, T. (2023, February 16). *How to make friends with your beautiful monsters.* Lion's Roar. https://www.lionsroar.com/how-to-make-friends-with-your-monsters/

Sevin. (2022, January 28). *The important philosophy of Buddhism: Compassion.* Medium. https://medium.com/@sushisev/buddhism-a-philosophy-of-compassion-1f5e6861b304

Sirimanne, C. (2016). Buddhism and women: The Dhamma has no gender. *Journal of International Women's Studies, 18*(1). https://vc.bridgew.edu/cgi/viewcontent.cgi?referer=&httpsredir=1&article=1923&context=jiws

Sivaraksa, S. (1998). Buddhism and human freedom. *Buddhist-Christian Studies, 18,* 63. JSTOR. https://doi.org/10.2307/1390436

Stamen Design. (2019). *The Ekmans' atlas of emotion.* The Ekmans' Atlas of Emotions. http://atlasofemotions.org/

Suni, E. (2021, February 23). *Revenge bedtime procrastination: Definition and psychology.* Sleep Foundation. https://www.sleepfoundation.org/sleep-hygiene/revenge-bedtime-procrastination

The 14th Dalai Lama. (2020, August 16). *The medicine of altruism.* The 14th Dalai Lama. https://www.dalailama.com/messages/world-peace/the-medicine-of-altruism

The 14th Dalai Lama. (2022, October 24). *Training the mind: Verse 2.* The 14th Dalai Lama. https://www.dalailama.com/teachings/training-the-mind/training-the-mind-verse-2

Awake Network. (2021). *Tsoknyi Rinpoche - befriending our "beautiful monsters": A guided practice for difficult emotions* [Video]. YouTube. https://www.youtube.com/watch?v=ldh6PeVtaQw&t=3s

The mindfulness of breathing. (n.d.). The Buddhist Centre. https://thebuddhistcentre.com/text/mindfulness-breathing

The Pluralism Project. (2023). *The Dharma: The teachings of the Buddha.* Pluralism; Harvard University. https://pluralism.org/the-dharma-the-teachings-of-the-buddha

The Yoga Nomads. (2022, July 14). *What is yoga nidra: A complete guide to the practice of yogic sleep.* The Yoga Nomads. https://www.theyoganomads.com/yoga-nidra/

Thich, N. H. (2023a). *Cultivating freedom.* Thich Nhat Hanh Foundation. https://thichnhathanhfoundation.org/blog/2018/7/6/cultivating-freedom

Thich, N. H. (2023b, January 17). *Thich Nhat Hanh on the practice of mindfulness.* Lion's Roar. https://www.lionsroar.com/mindful-living-thich-nhat-hanh-on-the-practice-of-mindfulness-march-2010/

Thich, N.H. (2007). *The art of power.* HarperOne.

Thich, N.H. (2021, March 9). *Thich Nhat Hanh on how to deal with strong emotions.* Plum Village. https://plumvillage.app/thich-nhat-hanh-on-how-to-deal-with-strong-emotions/

This is how Buddhist monks are taught to breathe. (2021, October 11). Motherhood Community. https://motherhoodcommunity.com/buddhist-monks-taught-breathe/

3 reasons why you should get some rest. (2021, July 15). Buddhability; Soka Gakkai Nichiren Buddhist. https://buddhability.org/practice/why-you-should-get-some-rest/

Timeline of world religions. (2022). Twinkl. https://www.twinkl.com/teaching-wiki/timeline-of-world-religions

12 Zen Buddhist practices that will change your life. (2021). The Denizen Co. https://www.thedenizenco.com/journal/zen-buddhist-practices

United Nations. (1948). *Universal declaration of human rights.* United Nations. https://www.un.org/en/about-us/universal-declaration-of-human-rights

Vanek Smith, S. (2020, January 23). *Buddhists, sociopaths, and the art of investing.* NPR. https://www.npr.org/2020/01/23/799051039/buddhists-sociopaths-and-the-art-of-investing

Weber, M. (2020, July 13). *Buddha on happiness.* Medium; Ascent Publication. https://medium.com/the-ascent/buddha-on-happiness-cd4cf5098e27

Wiebe, J. (2019, September 6). *When do fun distractions become unhealthy?* Talkspace. https://www.talkspace.com/blog/binge-distractions-unhealthy/

Wisdom. (2023). *Mind and emotions on the Buddhist path.* Wisdom Experience. https://wisdomexperience.org/wisdom-article/mind-emotions-buddhist-path/

Zandifar, M. (2018, October 21). *Buddhist psychology, love, and the avoidant attachment style.* The Happiness Clinic. https://www.thehappinessclinic.org/single-post/buddhist-psychology-love-avoidant-attachment-style#:~:text=The%20Buddhist%20concept%20of%20non

Printed by Amazon Italia Logistica S.r.l.
Torrazza Piemonte (TO), Italy